I0875885

THE SQE SURVIVAL GUIDE

Are you thinking about taking the SQE? The SQE Survival Guide covers everything you need to know about the SQE assessments and is full of helpful hints and tips for success. Written by expert legal educators, it takes you through the SQE process, alerting you to the common practical and academic pitfalls that trip up unsuspecting candidates, and giving you the tips needed to avoid them.

Of course, passing the SQE is only the start of your journey as a solicitor. To help you thrive in the legal profession, the book also includes advice on managing the start of your career journey and how to develop the necessary professional skills, attitudes, and behaviours that will power you through to the successful, happy, long-term career you deserve.

With advice and guidance on topics including emotional wellbeing, MCQ tactics, skills development, and career planning, this book will support and set you up for SQE success and to flourish as a legal professional.

Lucinda Bromfield is an Associate Professor of Educational Practice at BPP University Law School and a senior fellow of Advance HE. She has been designing and delivering professional legal education for over ten years. Her research interests include embedding life skills in learning and supporting wellbeing in legal education and the legal industry. Before joining BPP, she worked as a solicitor specialising in employment law.

Jonny Hurst is a former law firm partner who specialised in real estate before pivoting to legal education in 2007. He is the author of "Becoming a Lawyer," founder and presenter of the YouTube channel "SQE TV," and a longstanding Senior Lecturer at BPP University Law School, where he is now the Director of Outreach.

Kat Langley is an Assistant Professor of Criminal Law at Durham University. She has been researching and teaching law for the past nine years with a particular focus on professional skills and inclusivity. Prior to teaching, she trained at the Bar and specialised in representing immigration and asylum claimants.

Caroline Rayson is the Award Leader for the SQE1 Programmes at BPP University Law School. She worked for ten years as a corporate solicitor in the City before joining BPP in 2012 to train future solicitors in legal practice. She is a fellow of Advance HE.

THE SQE SURVIVAL GUIDE

Lucinda Bromfield, Jonny Hurst, Kat Langley and Caroline Rayson

Routledge
Taylor & Francis Group
LONDON AND NEW YORK

Designed cover image: iStock by Getty Images

First edition published 2027
by Routledge
4 Park Square, Milton Park, Abingdon, Oxon OX14 4RN

and by Routledge
605 Third Avenue, New York, NY 10158

Routledge is an imprint of the Taylor & Francis Group, an informa business

British Library Cataloguing-in-Publication Data
A catalogue record for this book is available from the British Library

Library of Congress Cataloging-in-Publication Data
Names: Bromfield, Lucinda author | Hurst, Jonny author | Langley, Katherine author | Rayson, Caroline author
Title: The SQE survival guide / Lucinda Bromfield, Jonny Hurst, Kat Langley, Caroline Rayson.
Description: 1. | New York : Routledge, 2026. | Includes bibliographical references and index. | Summary: – Provided by publisher.
Identifiers: LCCN 2026021789 | ISBN 9781041072706 hardback | ISBN 9781041072683 paperback | ISBN 9781003639671 ebook
Subjects: LCSH: Practice of law–Great Britain–Examinations, questions, etc. | Lawyers–Great Britain–Certification | Law–Study and teaching–Great Britain | Career development–Great Britain
Classification: LCC KD460 .B76 2026
LC record available at https://lccn.loc.gov/2026021789

ISBN: 9781041072706 (hbk)
ISBN: 9781041072683 (pbk)
ISBN: 9781003639671 (ebk)

DOI: 10.4324/9781003639671

Typeset in Sabon
by Deanta Global Publishing Services, Chennai, India

CONTENTS

PREFACE: WHO WE ARE AND WHY WE WROTE THIS BOOK

Authored by four legal academics with diverse professional backgrounds and a wide range of teaching, research, and practice experience, this guide brings together practical insight, academic rigour, and an honest understanding of the challenges students face. Collectively, we have supported learners at different stages of their legal journeys and across a variety of routes into the profession. That experience has shaped every chapter of this book.

With the Solicitors Qualifying Examination (SQE) bringing the biggest reform to professional legal qualifications in nearly 30 years, we've seen a concerning rise in the number of students who want to qualify as solicitors but are unaware of key elements of the SQE assessments. Unlike the LPC regime that preceded it, the SQE tests academic legal knowledge in detail across a broad range of areas, as well as testing knowledge of professional practice and procedures. In addition, the single best answer multiple-choice format of SQE1 is new to the majority of candidates, as are the examination procedures for both SQE1 and SQE2.

The aim of this *SQE Survival Guide* is simple: to help you navigate the qualification with confidence and clarity. It is designed to demystify the structure and demands of the SQE, explain what is expected of you, and provide realistic, student-focused strategies for preparation and success. We recognise that no two students are the same, and that circumstances, backgrounds, and preferred learning styles differ. This guide, therefore, seeks to be supportive, accessible, and practical rather than prescriptive.

Above all, we hope this book reassures you that, whilst the SQE is challenging, it is manageable – with the right guidance, preparation, and mindset.

The Solicitors Regulation Authority website is the best source of up-to-date information on the SQE. As this website is regularly updated, we have not included specific links within this book; it is important that you check the information on your own stage regularly (www.sqe.sra.org.uk).

Special thanks to Associate Professor of Legal Education Gillian Sproule and Deputy Director of Student Experience Laura Shuttleworth for their invaluable comments on the initial draft.

Lucinda Bromfield ORCiD: 0009-0000-7938-0648
Jonny Hurst ORCiD: 0009-0004-5970-2389
Kat Langley ORCiD: 0000-0002-2494-807X
Caroline Rayson ORCiD: 0009-0007-3493-5129

LIST OF ACRONYMS AND DEFINED TERMS

COLP:	Compliance Officer for Legal Practice
Day one solicitor:	Newly qualified solicitor on their first day working as a solicitor
CPE:	Common Professional Examination, an older name for the PGDL (see below)
FLK:	Functioning Legal Knowledge
FLK1:	Paper 1 of SQE1
FLK2:	Paper 2 of SQE1
GDL:	Graduate Diploma in Law, a law conversion course taught and assessed at Level 6 (see below)
GSA:	Graduate Solicitor Apprenticeship
LLB:	Bachelor of Laws, in this book, a degree in the law of England and Wales
LPC:	Legal Practice Course
MCQ:	Multiple-choice question
NQ:	Newly qualified
PGDL:	Postgraduate Diploma in Law, a law conversion course taught and assessed at Level 7, which is often pursued by non-law graduates seeking to qualify as barristers or solicitors
PQE:	Post-qualification experience
QWE:	Qualifying Work Experience
SBA MCQ:	Single best answer multiple-choice question
SLC:	Student Loans Company
SQE:	Solicitors Qualifying Examination, the centralised end point assessment future solicitors need to pass as part of their qualification journey

SQE1:	Multiple-choice SQE assessments, taken before SQE2
SQE2:	The skills SQE assessments, taken after passing SQE1
SRA:	Solicitors Regulation Authority

USEFUL WEB LINKS

- Accutrainee (Accutrainee, web page) https://accutrainee.com/ accessed 3 February 2026.
- AllAboutLaw (AllAboutLaw, web page) https://www.allaboutlaw.co.uk/ accessed 3 February 2026.
- Aspiring Solicitors (Aspiring Solicitors, web page) https://www.aspiringsolicitors.co.uk/ accessed 3 February 2026.
- Chambers Student (Chambers Student, web page) https://www.chambersstudent.co.uk/ accessed 3 February 2026.
- City of London Law Society (CLLS, web page) https://clls.org/ accessed 7 February 2026.
- Flex Legal (Flex Legal, web page) https://flex.legal/ accessed 3 February 2026.
- Government apprenticeship links (Gov.uk, web page) https://findapprenticeshiptraining.apprenticeships.education.gov.uk/courses/43 accessed 3 February 2026.
- HM Revenue and Customs (HMRC, web page) https://www.gov.uk accessed 1 August 2026.
- LawCareers.Net (LawCareers.Net, web page) https://www.lawcareers.net/ accessed 3 February 2026.
- Law Society (Law Society, web page) https://www.lawsociety.org.uk accessed 7 February 2026.
- Legal Cheek (Legal Cheek, web page) https://www.legalcheek.com/ accessed 3 February 2026.
- Legal Social Mobility Fund (Legal Social Mobility Fund, web page) https://www.legalsocialmobilityfund.org/ accessed 7 February 2026.
- Solicitors Regulation Authority (SRA, web page) https://www.sra.org.uk accessed 1 August 2026.
- SQE TV (SQE TV, Youtube) https://www.youtube.com/@SQETV accessed 9 February 2026.

- The Lawyer Portal (The Lawyer Portal, web page) https://www.thelawyerportal.com/ accessed 3 February 2026.
- Legal 500 Future Lawyers (The Legal 500, web page) https://www.legal500.com/future-lawyers/ accessed 3 February 2026.
- The Solicitors Qualifying Examination (SRA SQE, web page) https://sqe.sra.org.uk/ accessed 9 February 2026.
- The SQuarE Route (The SQuarE Route, web page) https://thesqeroute.com/ accessed 3 February 2026.

ILLUSTRATIONS

Figures

Tables

INTRODUCTION TO THE SQE ROUTE AND QUALIFICATION

Background

The Solicitors Qualifying Examination (SQE) was introduced by the Solicitors Regulation Authority (SRA) in 2021 to replace the outgoing Legal Practice Course (LPC). With very few exceptions, all future solicitors now need to pass the SQE in order to qualify as a solicitor.

We have written this book because, unlike the LPC, which was a linear and relatively simple pathway to understand, qualifying as a solicitor via the SQE route is, for many candidates, significantly more complex to navigate.

The SQE comes with its own language. You will soon become accustomed to a string of three-letter acronyms, such as "FLK" (Functioning Legal Knowledge assessed on the SQE) and "QWE" (the on-the-job Qualifying Work Experience you need to qualify). We will introduce you to all of these terms to help you map the start of your career (see also "List of acronyms and terms," page ix).

Much of the profession is still getting to grips with the SQE. So, you're in good company if you have been wondering where to start researching your options. We hope that by the time you finish reading this book, the SQE pathway will be a little less daunting. Along the way, we will share practical tips and tools to help you prepare. Whilst we can't guarantee a pass, you will certainly be better equipped to tackle the exam and navigate the key decisions every candidate faces on their journey to qualification.

Pathways to qualification

To qualify as a solicitor via the SQE, the three main hurdles most candidates need to clear are:

- An undergraduate degree;
- Passing the SQE; and
- Completing two years of Qualifying Work Experience (QWE).

DOI: 10.4324/9781003639671-1

We will consider each of these in detail in later chapters, but it is worth noting at this introductory stage that the SRA does not regulate the order in which you choose to complete each of these three requirements. Indeed, it is possible to work towards some of them simultaneously, which means there is no prescribed order for completing them.

So, one of the big advantages of the SQE regime is the flexibility it gives to candidates, which means that you can tailor your SQE journey to best suit your personal circumstances. To illustrate this, the figures below set out a few of the more popular ways candidates navigate the SQE.

This is the simplest SQE pathway to understand. It mirrors the traditional LPC journey to qualification, as you complete all your studies before commencing the work experience element. It is the route that sponsoring law firms still usually adopt for their future trainees, and it is also popular with many self-funding students who prefer to get their education "out of the way" before starting working life. It also works well for candidates who have recently completed an undergraduate law degree or conversion course and wish to study for the SQE part time alongside full-time employment in a non-QWE role.

Because the SRA does not prescribe the order in which a candidate completes their SQE and QWE, a wide range of other routes to qualification via the SQE have emerged. In particular, it is now possible to start your QWE before commencing your SQE journey, which is the route taken by many paralegals.

The flexibility of the SQE regime means that candidates are not obliged to undertake their QWE at any particular point in the process. In practice, some candidates who have worked as paralegals accrue the whole of their two years of QWE before they even begin the SQE,

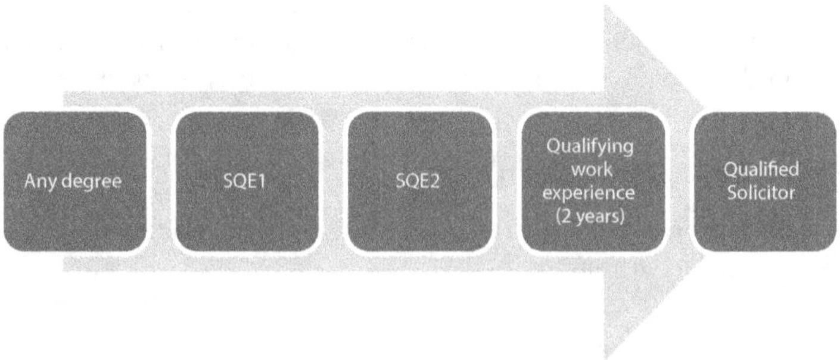

FIGURE 0.1 "Traditional" pathway to qualification via the SQE.

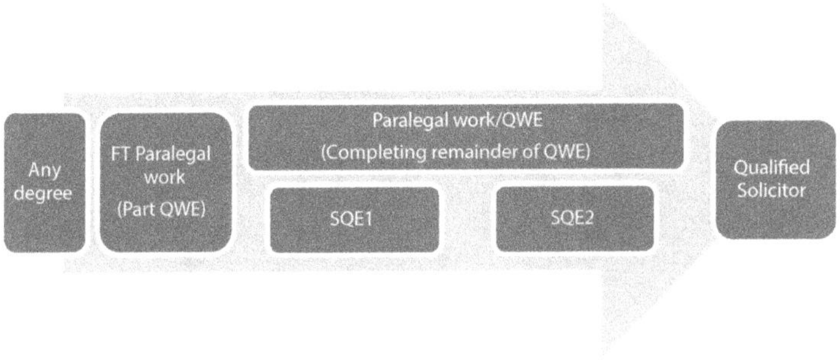

FIGURE 0.2 Paralegal pathway to qualification.

whilst others may start their SQE preparation partway through. This is illustrated in Figure 0.2.

Many paralegals choose to work full time and undertake their SQE assessment preparation around their day job. As such, they often enrol on part-time courses or choose an SQE "test prep" solution that they can study more flexibly.

As a variation on Figure 0.2, to illustrate the flexibility of the SQE pathway, Figure 0.3 shows that it is possible to start working in the legal profession and your SQE journey at the same time. This model is popular with self-funding candidates who choose to work full time and study part time in order to help finance their SQE journey. It is also popular with candidates who choose, at least initially, to commit only to studying towards SQE1, which provides them with greater flexibility in terms of when and how they start preparing for SQE2.

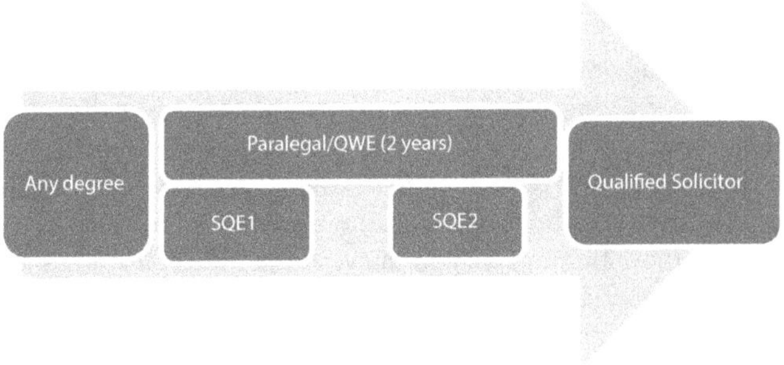

FIGURE 0.3 "Earning and learning" pathway to qualification.

FIGURE 0.4 Graduate Solicitor Apprenticeship pathway to qualification.

Graduate Solicitor Apprenticeships (GSAs) are another way you can be sponsored by a legal employer (Figure 0.4). In contrast to the "traditional" SQE pathway shown in Figure 0.1, which most other sponsored trainees will follow, graduate solicitor apprentices are employed from the start of their qualification journey: they will, in most cases, work for the employer four days per week, and on the fifth, they are released to undertake their SQE training and preparation for their SQE assessments. The work element is, effectively, the apprentice's QWE.

GSAs have financial benefits to both the apprentice and the employer. For the apprentice, you are "earning and learning" and will not have to pay for your SQE preparation course or assessments. For employers, government funding for such apprentices' SQE training is available by drawing down from their previous apprenticeship levy payments, which each employer will have paid if their annual payroll exceeds £3 million.

Whilst this pathway is still available, changes to the apprenticeship funding rules, effective from 1 January 2026, mean that employers cannot draw down the funding for new apprentices who start their GSA over the age of 21. This does not prevent employers from hiring new GSAs over the age of 21 if they are prepared to cover the full SQE training and assessment costs (like they would do for a "regular" sponsored trainee). However, whilst some employers have indicated that they would still take on GSAs over the age of 21 (and cover all their SQE costs), these funding changes may, in the future, lead to a reduction in the number of GSA places being offered nationally.

One other route to qualification is the Level 7 solicitor apprenticeship which is for candidates who start the apprenticeship aged 18 to 21. In most cases, this is a six-year programme (which entails a weekly

FIGURE 0.5 Level 7 solicitor apprenticeship pathway to qualification.

pattern of four days' work in the profession, with a fifth day devoted to legal studies). In the last two years of such an apprenticeship, the apprentice prepares for and sits the SQE assessments whilst continuing to work in the office for four days per week. As with GSAs, the work element for Level 7 solicitor apprentices is, effectively, the QWE.

This is a relatively new route and has attracted a lot of interest from candidates who are happy to trade the "university experience" for debt-free training and strong prospects for a permanent role upon qualification.

What is the SQE? (An overview)

To understand the SQE further, it is useful to have a basic understanding of how the outgoing LPC was regulated.

Centralised assessments

The SQE is just the final endpoint assessment. In contrast, the LPC was both a course *and* an assessment. LPC training providers would write their own courses, as well as set and mark their own exams, which were overseen by the SRA's external examiners. The SRA believed that this would produce an element of consistency in delivery and quality across all LPC training providers.

After 30 years of the LPC, the SRA concluded that some LPC courses were considered better/inferior to others, and some were harder/easier to pass. Consequently, the SRA became concerned that the brand and integrity of the qualification itself might fall into disrepute unless the LPC was reformed or abolished altogether.

So, when designing the SQE regime, the SRA decided to revert to a single centralised assessment which all candidates sit, and they appointed Kaplan as its independent examination provider to write, mark, and administer all SQE assessments.

No prescribed way to prepare for the SQE

The SRA does not regulate how candidates prepare themselves to sit the SQE. As such, the SRA does not oversee the content of any SQE preparation courses or materials, nor does it require any parties who offer such courses or materials to be validated or checked in any way.

TAKE A MOMENT ...

As the regulator has decided not to exert any form of quality control over SQE training products, this has given rise to an explosion of SQE apps, materials, and courses on the market. Prospective candidates should exercise caution before paying for anything (however low the price may be) from sources, especially online vendors, whose credentials and qualities are often impossible to verify.

We expect that the pass rates of students who study with particular SQE training providers will, increasingly, become a critical metric to compare providers and their courses, not least because the pass rate for SQE1 first sitters has been as low as 46% and has only averaged a little above 50% since the start of the SQE regime. Unfortunately, the collection and publication of this data have not been as straightforward as the SRA and the market would have hoped; the reasons for which we will explain later (see "SQE pass rates," Part 1, pages 20–22).

Introduction to the SQE syllabus

A crucial aspect of the SQE regime is that it re-examines candidates on the core subjects they studied during their law degree or law conversion course. In fact, up to half of the questions in SQE1 will be in the areas of Tort, Contract, Criminal, Trusts, Land, Public law, and the Legal System. As such, regardless of the route they have taken to the SQE, all candidates must commit time to updating/refreshing and revising their knowledge of these subjects. Most of the other half of the assessment specification is made up of a series of "practice subjects," including Business Law and Practice, Property Practice, Dispute Resolution, Professional Conduct, Wills and the Administration of Estates and Criminal Law and Practice.

One of the benefits of the SQE regime is that it allows you to access different types of training courses and materials. The content of some will be exclusively focused on preparing you for the SQE, whereas others will include additional skills and training in specialist practice areas that are outside the scope of the relatively narrow SQE curriculum.

TAKE A MOMENT ...

Some candidates treat the SQE as the "minimum floor," not the "maximum ceiling" in terms of the knowledge and training which they believe they will need in the early part of their careers. They believe more training now will enable them to "hit the ground running" on day one of their QWE. Others wish to just focus on the SQE for now and expect to pick up specialist practice-area knowledge during their QWE.

Which type of candidate are you?

Introduction to the SQE assessments

We will spend a great deal of time in Parts 2 and 3 discussing the nature of the SQE1 and SQE2 assessments and how to best prepare for them. For now, here is a quick overview.

SQE1 overview

SQE1 is assessed by way of 360 multiple-choice questions, which students sit in two parts on any two days in consecutive weeks in either January or July each year (known as FLK1 and FLK2). The MCQs cover all the knowledge and practice areas referred to above, which are assessed on a "closed-book" basis at a Pearson Vue test centre.

SQE2 overview

If you pass (or are exempt from) SQE1, you are eligible to sit SQE2. There are four opportunities to sit SQE2 each year: January/February, April/May, July/August, and October/November. SQE2 consists of 16 mini assessments (which the SRA refers to as "stations"). Twelve of the stations cover the written skills of Case and Matter Analysis, Legal Writing, Legal Drafting and Legal Research. The remaining four test your oral skills of Advocacy and Interviewing.

It is important to understand that SQE2 candidates must retain their FLK from SQE1, as half of the SQE2 marks are awarded for knowledge of the law in which the relevant skill is being assessed.

Introduction to QWE

One of the major benefits of the SQE regime is that candidates don't have to complete their two years of QWE in one block of two years with a single employer. In fact, they can accrue QWE with up to four employers, and as you will have noted from Figures 0.1–0.5, QWE can be accumulated before you start your SQE journey, whilst you are on it, after you've passed your SQE exams, or any combination of the above!

This means there are multiple opportunities to acquire and complete QWE, particularly because the nature of the job and the opportunities you have in the role are more important than the job title. Consequently, career paralegals may not need to acquire any further junior roles before qualifying, as the work they have done to date may amount to at least two years of QWE.

Many candidates still sign up for two years of QWE with a single employer, commonly referred to as a "training contract," even though the rules relating to it are very different from those for training contracts under the old LPC regime.

We will explore QWE in more detail in Part 4 (see "QWE," pages 129–135).

1

IS THE SQE RIGHT FOR YOU?

What do you need to know if you are thinking about starting the SQE?

Are you really sure you want to be a solicitor?

Unless you *really* want to be a solicitor, don't do the SQE!

Sounds obvious, doesn't it? But there are plenty of candidates currently on SQE journeys who have only a limited understanding of the career they're signing up for. This is echoed by graduate recruiters who say they read far too many bland answers to the question: "Why do you want to be a solicitor?"

Being a solicitor is a great career for the right person. But how do you know if you're *that* person?

There are as many "correct answers" to "why you want to be a solicitor?" as there are good SQE candidates. Whilst you might have much in common with your peers, your personal journey to this point, interests, and motivations are unique. But if the first time you have properly thought about why you want to become a solicitor is when you apply for an SQE course or complete your first application to a law firm, you may struggle during the recruitment process.

Do you have the resilience to succeed?

Even the strongest of SQE candidates will face a succession of bumps on the road, such as receiving a series of rejections from employers. Some will fail an SQE assessment, and many will face financial challenges. Your physical and mental health could also be put to the test at times. We don't recommend starting an SQE journey unless you are absolutely sure that the exams and the recruitment process, with all the uncertainty they entail, are for you. Your journey needs to start

DOI: 10.4324/9781003639671-2

by thoroughly considering your suitability for what can be a long and winding road to qualification and the career of a solicitor itself. It's never too early to consider the realities of what you will be signing up for.

In order to articulate why you want to be a solicitor, you need to spend time thinking and researching:

- what *your* career as a solicitor *might* look like;
- why *you* think *you* are suited to the profession; and
- what will continue to motivate *you to* study, pass your exams, and thrive as a trainee and beyond?

This exercise doesn't simply require you to carry out the research. You might have a clear understanding of what being a solicitor involves, and perhaps you have the potential to develop the right skill set. But unless you can demonstrate to others that you have the motivation and drive to achieve these goals, any perceived lack of enthusiasm may be viewed adversely in the recruitment process. Employers like to see evidence of a "spark" that they hope they will be able to "light" once you join them.

TAKE A MOMENT ...

You owe it to yourself to start properly working out whether you want to be a solicitor well before you start your SQE journey. If you shy away from it now or have difficulty convincing yourself that it is the career for you, how will you know you're on the right pathway? How will you convince an interviewer?

In order to further explore your personal motivations, you might want to think about who and/or what may have inspired your interest in practising as a solicitor. If you are already a law student, this ought to be one stage further from the reason(s) why you originally chose to *study* law. What you need to project is more than having a mere curiosity for the law. It's more about having a genuine interest in the vocation of legal practice and understanding why it might excite you.

And you don't get this from watching *Suits* or other legal dramas, or suddenly discover your motivation in the time it takes to complete an online application. Most candidates who secure a training contract will have worked this out by committing time and thought to their career over a sustained period. But if you sleepwalk into the SQE and the recruitment process without having done the groundwork, the chances are you won't end up with the career you thought you aspired to.

Do I need to know what type of solicitor I'm going to be before committing to the SQE?

There will be some SQE candidates who have "known" they wanted to be a criminal lawyer since they read *To Kill a Mockingbird* or some other work of fiction. Others will have a very clear idea that they want to work in a particular legal sector (e.g., corporate law) but are less sure about their future practice area. And there are many others, perhaps the majority, who will have conflicting ideas, or perhaps no idea at all of where they see themselves in legal practice.

Does it matter? The short answer is "no"! If you have a more flexible approach to your legal destination at the time you commit to the SQE, that's fine, as long as you are actively working out what types of employers, legal sectors, and practice areas interest you. It's an evolving process of elimination, and different candidates will work out which practice areas/types of firms and so on, interest them at different stages of the process.

For those who have more fixed ideas, we would always encourage you to keep an open mind. This has two advantages: it means having a larger pool of potential employers to apply to and areas within which you can work, and that you are open to discovering a love of a type of law you didn't consider, or didn't even know existed until you were exposed to it.

We regularly hear from alumni who practise in areas they never imagined they would get into when they started studing for their professional qualifications. The most extreme example that comes to mind is a student determined to practise immigration law who now works in banking and trusts, having discovered a deep interest in both during her studies.

Ask yourself whether you've done the equivalent of stopping halfway down the menu in a restaurant and then giving the waiter your order without exploring the rest of the dishes available. You may have made a premature decision and have missed out on a more appetising dish. The result? You end up with the professional equivalent of "food envy" when you later discover what everyone else has opted for!

TAKE A MOMENT ...

Once you have decided that becoming a solicitor is the career for you, make every effort to develop an idea of why you might want to work at a particular type of legal employer or in a particular sector. Even if you honestly think "I just want to qualify," at least make sure that the opportunities and experiences you apply for will interest you and play to your strengths.

QWE strategy

In Part 4, you will learn a lot more about QWE – what it is and how to acquire it. If you don't have QWE or a training contract already, you should read that chapter at the earliest possible opportunity because anyone embarking on an SQE journey should already be well on the way to working out the QWE strategy which is most likely to work for them.

Your SQE prep strategy

As well as being sure why you want to qualify as a solicitor and having a clear QWE strategy, you also need to research and ultimately decide how you will prepare for your SQE assessments.

If you are sponsored by a large firm or a solicitor apprentice, the decision will be made for you by your future employer: they will direct you to a particular SQE training provider, not least because they will be paying for the course and/or your SQE assessment fees.

It is less common for smaller firms that offer training contracts or QWE to fund (in part or the whole of) your SQE studies or exam fees. A small number may pay for part of the course fees, some may provide you with an interest-free loan, but most will leave it to their future trainees to finance the whole of their SQE journey, including the cost of the assessments.

There is no hard and fast rule as to what an employer will pay for; each will have their own policy, which is usually set out on its recruitment web pages.

If you are contemplating self-funding most or all of your SQE journey like well over 50% of candidates, there are three questions you should ask yourself:

- What type of SQE preparation course(s) (if any) do I want to take?
- Where do I want to study?
- How will I finance my studies and the SQE exam fees?

Types of SQE preparation

Do you need to buy an SQE preparation course at all?

In theory – and we stress, in theory – provided you have an undergraduate degree in any subject (it doesn't even have to be a law degree!), you could read a few books, practise a set of MCQs, and then book yourself in for SQE1. Good luck! But don't expect to pass!

Although it is possible to pass the SQE without any formal tuition, the vast majority of candidates, including almost all of those with QWE training contracts at leading law firms, could not possibly teach themselves everything they need for the SQE and still achieve their potential in the assessments.

Most candidates need a comprehensive programme of learning to maximise their chances of passing with the highest marks they are capable of achieving. This group probably includes you and almost every other prospective solicitor you know.

TAKE A MOMENT ...

There is a wide range of options for candidates looking to prepare for the SQE, which offer flexibility and choice. When you are planning the best way for *you* to prepare for the SQE, consider how you will strike a balance between the cost of a given preparation route and the benefit you can expect it to bring you in terms of success in the assessments and at the start of your career in practice. Take time to undertake your research properly, considering your needs, lifestyle, and resources.

Non-law graduates and the SQE

Unlike the Bar Standards Board, which requires non-law graduates studying for the English and Welsh Bar to have passed a recognised law conversion course like the Postgraduate Diploma in Law (PGDL), the SRA does not stipulate such a requirement for non-law graduates who wish to qualify as solicitors. This provides a very mixed message to such candidates, as many don't appreciate that without a PGDL (or equivalent), they will not be on a level playing field with Bachelor of Laws (LLB) and PGDL graduates, who will have already learned around half of the FLK required for SQE1.

The SRA says that it will not police a candidate's learning journey to the SQE assessments: so if a candidate feels ready to sit SQE1 without undertaking a full law conversion course, they should be given the opportunity to do so. However, since a significant majority of non-law graduates who aspire to become solicitors are recent graduates with little or no legal or business experience, we recommend that they undertake a comprehensive law conversion course like the PGDL before they start their SQE preparation.

The SRA has explained its position on *Legal Cheek* as follows:

> We're not saying that a non-law graduate has to do the [P]GDL but we wouldn't imagine that a non-law graduate would attempt SQE1 without having done some sort of training. ... that doesn't have to be the [P]GDL or CPE. It could be a different sort of course provided by a different sort of provider. It could be self-study. It could be a correspondence course. You make the decision about what works for you to enable you to prepare you to sit SQE1.

It is, perhaps, unfortunate that the SRA doesn't steer more positively recent non-law graduates towards comprehensive law conversion courses. Consequently, it has been left to providers and commentators to unravel the misconceptions many non-law graduates have acquired and to explain the value and importance of a PGDL.

TAKE A MOMENT ...

If you are a non-law graduate considering an SQE preparation course, you need to understand how prepared a PGDL (or equivalent) will make you for the start of your SQE journey, as opposed to a cheaper, quicker crammer course. Such courses usually fall short of what most non-law graduates need, and when you consider that you only have three attempts at any SQE assessment in a six-year period, cutting corners with your legal education is a significant risk.

This is your career we're talking about. It's not a race to qualify!

The range of SQE preparation options

By not prescribing how candidates prepare for the SQE, the SRA has created a market for SQE courses and materials in which there is a wide range of study options on offer.

In general, there are five types of SQE "delivery mode" for which you can pay:

1. *Regular in-person face-to-face teaching* supported by online learning platforms and physical and digital materials.
2. *Regular live online teaching* supported by online learning platforms and physical and digital materials.
3. *A digital application with limited live teaching touchpoints.*
4. *A digital application with no tutor support.*
5. *Self-study options* are a mix of physical and online materials that candidates can mix and match across different suppliers.

There are online courses ... and there are online courses!

Live face-to-face teaching (Option 1) continues to be a popular option with the majority of leading law firms who sponsor their future trainees, as well as a significant proportion of self-funding candidates. However, online and self-study options are the only practical solutions for candidates who do not live or work close enough to an SQE provider to attend in person. They are also attractive if you are time-poor or require greater flexibility. For example, you may need to travel regularly or have family or caring commitments. And, of course, these options cut out the commute, thereby saving you travel costs.

The range of online and self-study options is vast. No two are identical, so if you're seriously contemplating online training, it is important you first identify and, if necessary, prioritise what it is you are looking for before coming up with a shortlist of online/self-study options which best suit your learning style and your pocket and strike a reasonable balance between the two. In doing the research, you need to ensure you fully understand what you will and will not be paying for and, ultimately, be comfortable with what you are not going to get.

Live online teaching courses

The more expensive online SQE courses tend to be the ones which mirror the in-person SQE learning experience at the same provider, with a significant amount of regular live teaching – hence the greater cost.

Live teaching is the mode of learning with which almost all learners are most familiar. A significant additional benefit, which candidates sometimes underestimate, is the ability to have their understanding instantly validated (or challenged) by their tutors and peers. Many SQE candidates prefer to study this way because the sociable interaction makes the process more enjoyable and the content more memorable.

If you enjoy regularly participating in classroom discussions (which we would always encourage), it is likely that you will develop your understanding of the many complex SQE concepts more quickly and comprehensively in a live online classroom as opposed to most self-study options. So, if you need to study online, value these benefits and are happy to pay a premium for it, a live online course with regular teaching might be best aligned to your learning preferences.

Other online and self-study options

Some candidates, however, need even greater flexibility because, for example, they cannot commit to regularly scheduled live online teaching workshops, or their learning preference is more suited to self-studying at their own pace. In addition, the ability to pause your studies when work or life gets in the way and to accelerate them when you have more time also has its attractions, especially if you have unpredictable family or work commitments. Indeed, a significant proportion of candidates who choose these options are in full-time employment.

If any of the above situations resonate with you, you may be better suited to one of options 3, 4, or 5. The candidates who tend to perform better with one of these options tend to be the ones who are naturally well-organised, are confident they will have the drive and discipline to commit to in-depth self-study over a sustained period, and are less likely to need regular tutor or peer support.

In addition, some candidates are more naturally suited to self-study, especially if they have proven to themselves in previous studies that they are able to be largely self-reliant and, when doing so, have achieved excellent results.

Choosing the right course for you

As you are beginning to appreciate, the SQE is a very challenging assessment, not just in terms of the complexity of the content, but also because of the sheer volume you need to absorb, retain and apply in your assessments. Consequently, when it comes to your SQE preparation, whichever study option you choose, it is likely that there will be times when you struggle to grasp some of the concepts or feel completely overwhelmed. The first thing to note is that these emotions are perfectly normal as they are experienced by almost all SQE candidates at some time or another, so you will not be alone!

One of the secrets to success is how you manage these moments, which will, at least in part, depend on the type of SQE preparation you choose and the extent of the support on hand.

Irrespective of their choice of study option, candidates who struggle with the MCQs in SQE1 tend to be the ones who don't progress beyond "surface learning" and don't appreciate the depth of understanding they need to arrive at the correct answer for the right reasons. A tutor will be able to pick you up on this in a live, taught class, whereas the onus is almost exclusively on each student if they choose an online or self-study option with little or no tutor input. If you are confident that you have the ability to consistently analyse each concept and MCQ you encounter with the necessary rigour, self-study might be a viable option for you. However, if you think you may need more regular guidance or reassurance, you may be better suited to a live teaching option.

TAKE A MOMENT ...

Make sure you only commit to an SQE preparation option which aligns with your learning preferences, your personal circumstances, and is the one you believe will maximise your chances of passing SQE1. If you choose an online or self-study option, make sure you fully understand and are comfortable with your future learning environment and the extent of the support available to you, especially if you are not considering a live teaching option.

Choosing an SQE preparation course: Other factors

When choosing an SQE course, you also need to consider:

Full-time or part-time study?

This is very much a personal decision and will normally be determined by whether you want to or need to undertake paid work alongside your SQE studies and what other responsibilities you have (e.g., caring for dependants). Full-time courses will often be around half as long as the part-time equivalent offered by the same provider. Whilst completing a part-time course will tend to take you longer to complete your SQE journey, one of the benefits is that you will normally be able to spread your course payments over a longer period.

Where do I want to study?

Our advice, if you are choosing face-to-face study, is, wherever possible, to study in or close to the area where you wish to start your career, especially if you have not yet secured QWE or a training contract, because it will be easier for you to access the networking and career development opportunities you are interested in.

The trade-off for some candidates is to study online or at the law school closest to their family home in order to minimise overall costs, which is likely to be much cheaper, as most will only occasionally travel to employability events.

Do I want pure SQE test prep or more comprehensive career preparation?

Most SQE preparation options are exclusively focused on preparing you for the SQE assessments. However, as we have explained earlier, there are others which also deliver extremely useful specialist practice area knowledge and skills training beyond the SQE syllabus. These more comprehensive courses tend to be master's versions of SQE preparation courses, which have the added benefit of qualifying for postgraduate funding for eligible students (see also this chapter, "Financing your SQE course fees: Master's loan," page 28). Such additional learning can also give candidates a head start in their QWE if they are placed in a department which specialises in one or more of the practice areas they have studied. It can also give candidates a slight edge in the recruitment process, as they will be able to reference it to demonstrate their interest in and commitment to a particular sector.

However, the extra time and cost which an SQE master's will entail will not usually be appropriate for paralegals and some other candidates who view the SQE more as a hurdle to overcome in order to qualify, rather than a significant part of their legal education. That said, wrapping up your SQE preparation in a master's can be the simplest and most cost-effective way for some domestic students to finance a significant proportion of their training. However, most candidates will need to look at other options if they wish to avoid adding to their long-term student debt or are ineligible for master's funding.

Does the SRA publish a list of "recommended" SQE training providers?

The short answer is "no." As we have already mentioned, the SRA only regulates the end-point assessment (i.e., the SQE), not the journey you take to get there. This means the SRA does not endorse or oversee any SQE training provider, their courses, or materials.

The SRA has, instead, provided an *SQE training and course finder* on their website, which is an online tool containing information about SQE providers. The finder allows you to search and filter the list of training providers and their courses/materials by way of:

- Assessment covered (i.e., SQE1, SQE2, or both)
- Delivery mode – broadly matching the list of delivery modes we have explained on page 15 (see "The range of SQE preparation options")
- Cost range
- Course suitability (e.g., for independent learners, international students, non-law graduates)
- Course length
- Availability of funding support (e.g., scholarships and bursaries)
- Inclusion of assessment preparation (e.g., sample questions and mock assessments)

It is extremely important to highlight the SRA's caveat in relation to the providers listed, whom they describe as "organisations who have asked to be included but ... [they are] not verified by us. It is not a comprehensive or definitive list of organisations."

TAKE A MOMENT ...

Whilst the SRA's *SQE training and course finder* contains all the leading SQE training providers and many others, candidates should not assume that by virtue of being on the list, it is somehow a badge of quality or approval by the SRA. It simply isn't. As helpful as the list might be in identifying a large proportion of the training options in the SQE preparation market, it doesn't remove the need for candidates to fully research the pros and cons of each, well beyond the filters which the tool offers. Choosing the best SQE training option for you is much more nuanced, as you will now be appreciating.

SQE pass rates

Shortly after the results are released for each SQE assessment, the SRA publishes a detailed statistical report. These reports contain really useful information about how well candidates have performed, including the overall pass rate, the first-sitters' pass rate, and how well candidates have done in the various practice areas and skills.

There were a number of transitional reasons for some pass rates in the first two years of the new qualification regime. As they will be of little interest to most readers, we have not included them in Tables 1.1 and 1.2, which show the overall pass rates for SQE1 and SQE2 from January 2023 – January 2026.

TABLE 1.1 SQE1 pass rates January 2023 – January 2026 (table collated from the SRA's SQE assessment reports).

Sitting	All sitters	First sitters
January 2023	51%	54%
July 2023	53%	56%
January 2024	56%	59%
July 2024	44%	48%
January 2025	56%	60%
July 2025	41%	46%
January 2026	53%	58%

TABLE 1.2 SQE2 pass rates January 2023 – January 2026 (table collated from the SRA's SQE assessment reports).

Sitting	All sitters	First sitters
April 2023	77%	80%
July 2023	79%	82%
October 2023	64%	69%
January 2024	73%	76%
April 2024	79%	81%
July 2024	74%	77%
October 2024	81%	83%
January 2025	75%	77%
April 2025	82%	84%
July 2025	76%	79%
October 2025	78%	79%
January 2026	80%	79%

With SQE1 pass rates ranging between 46% and 60% for first sitters, broadly averaging in the early 50s, this is likely to be the first academic assessment most readers have had a serious chance of failing. So, self-funding candidates may be best advised to choose the study option and course which they believe will give them the best chance of passing first time, rather than the course which they will be able to complete the soonest.

The pass rates for SQE2 are much higher than SQE1 because you have to pass SQE1 before you can sit SQE2. Consequently, SQE2 cohorts will, overall, always be academically stronger than SQE1 cohorts.

We have also consolidated the pass rate data for a selection of diversity categories in Table 1.3, focusing on the three most significant

TABLE 1.3 SQE1 pass rates for first sitters January 2023 – January 2026 by diversity category (table collated from the SRA's SQE assessment reports).

Diversity category	Group 1	Group 2	Group 3
Ethnicity	Asian/Asian British: 39%–56%	Black/Black British: 28%–44%	White: 55%–76%
Disability according to the Equality Act 2010?	Yes: 46%–67%	No: 45%–66%	Prefer not to say: 54%–76%
Sex	Female: 43%–63%	Male: 49%–71%	Prefer not to say: 62%–78%
Age	16–24: 48%–66%	25–34: 47%–70%	35–44: 41%–57%
Did either parent attend university before you were 18?	Yes: 51%–70%	No: 41%–60%	Prefer not to say: 41%–69%
Undergraduate degree classification	1st class: 67%–84%	2:1: 46%–64%	2:2: 19%–35%
Type of school	State: 44%–64%	Independent/ fee paying: 54%–74%	Outside UK: 43%–63%
Occupation of the main household earner when you were 14	Professional: 50%-69%	Intermediate: 41%–61%	Working class: 41%–60%
First language (data only available from January 2024)	English: 48%–68%	Other: 37%–63%	Unknown: 32%–61%

groups each time. Whilst being a selective data set, with some data omitted for brevity, a number of significant themes have started to emerge, especially where the SRA has cut the data with reference to different aspects of candidates' backgrounds.

What themes have emerged from this data?

Ethnicity

There is a troubling and significant attainment gap between the SQE outcomes for white candidates and those from minority ethnic backgrounds. In 2021, the SRA commissioned the University of Exeter to research this in relation to the outgoing LPC and GDL, which revealed similar differentials. The final report, published in 2024, identified that the causes are numerous and complex, often reflecting the social disadvantage which candidates have experienced because of early life factors and socioeconomic and educational disadvantage. Sadly, the data do not appear to suggest that the SQE has moved the dial towards anything approaching parity.

Disability

Overall, candidates with a disability are passing SQE1 at around the same rate as others. However, we believe that, for the sake of transparency, this data needs to be broken down further in order to establish whether any particular groups within the disabled community are not performing as well as others, so any disadvantage can be reviewed and, if necessary, addressed.

Sex

The male pass rate for SQE1 has consistently been higher than for female candidates, whereas their pass rates are very similar for SQE2. This might suggest that the way single best answer MCQs are drafted in the SQE is better suited to the male brain. Or perhaps it might have something to do with the fact that many more females (around 65%) sit the SQE than males (around 33%). Further research needs to be undertaken to explain this disparity. Remedial steps will need to be undertaken by the SRA if the conclusion is that the SQE1 assessment unfairly discriminates against female candidates.

Age

Candidates in their 20s and 30s seem to be passing at broadly the same rate and in higher proportions compared with older candidates.

Social mobility factors: Parents' university status and occupation, candidates' schooling

Candidates with at least one parent who went to university, those with parents in professional occupations, and candidates who went to independent or fee-paying schools are outperforming their peers from more modest social and educational backgrounds. This echoes the point made above in relation to minority ethnic candidates, although the attainment gap in relation to these social mobility factors is not quite as stark.

Undergraduate degree classification

Those with first-class degrees are significantly outperforming those with 2:1s, who themselves are doing much better than candidates with a 2:2, with, on average, only a quarter of the latter passing SQE1 first time. This clearly supports the SRA's view that past educational attainment is the best indicator of a candidate's prospects of success in the SQE. That said, it is still troubling that the data show that 16%–33% of SQE1 first sitters with first-class degrees are failing at least one SQE1 assessment.

English as a first language

Given that a strong command of the written and spoken word is the most important currency of any practising lawyer, those candidates who were brought up with English as an additional language are, as a whole, finding SQE1 more challenging. There is a significant attainment gap in the SQE2 data for such candidates as well.

It is important that future candidates don't look at this data and worry that it will define their SQE1 journey. It shouldn't do so at all, because candidates from all backgrounds are passing. But the data, especially the low overall pass rate for SQE1, should act as a warning to all candidates, whatever your background, that the SQE is an assessment regime which needs to be taken seriously from the moment you start researching your options all the way to the end of your final assessment.

Pass rates of SQE training providers

When the SRA launched the SQE in 2021, they committed to publishing pass rate data by training provider. However, despite separately assuring the market that it would publish such information by the end of each of 2023, 2024, and 2025, the SRA has still not, at the time of publication, shared any pass rate data attributed to particular training providers. This is despite the fact that all stakeholders, especially future candidates, have been consistently calling for access to such critical information before they commit to investing in their SQE journey.

In a statement released in late 2025 on the subject of training provider-attributed pass rates, the SRA admitted that they "have not had confidence in the quality of the data collected. Therefore, publishing this data would risk misleading candidates." So, sadly, the earliest the SRA might publish providers' pass rate data is in late 2026, but more realistically, some time in 2027.

Only a very limited number of SQE training providers regularly published their pass rates in the first four years of the SQE. They did so based on data they collected from their students who were happy to share their results. During the same period, we expect some (if not all) other providers have been similarly surveying their students but have chosen not to publish their data.

On a related point, you may also be surprised to learn that the SRA and Kaplan did not, for the first four years of the SQE, share individual candidates' results with their training providers and, at the time of publication, have no plans of doing so.

There is little doubt that a training provider's pass rates should be factored into most candidates' decision-making process to purchase a particular SQE training product. But until the SRA publishes data which it and the market can rely on, candidates will be left to form their own conclusions in relation to whether a provider chooses to publish (or not publish) their pass rate data and the reliability of the pass rate claims of the few who do.

Challenges for neurodiverse candidates (and others)

The SQE offers a new, standardised route to qualification, but for *neurodiverse candidates* – including those with dyslexia, dyspraxia,

ADHD, autism, or other cognitive differences – it can pose distinctive challenges. Understanding these early helps candidates plan effectively, access support, and perform at their best.

Cognitive and processing demands

Both stages of the SQE test sustained concentration and working memory under significant time pressure.

- *SQE1*, with its multiple-choice questions, requires rapid reading, comprehension, and decision-making. For those with slower processing speeds or reading difficulties, this can be mentally exhausting.
- *SQE2* involves live assessments of advocacy, interviewing, and writing skills, which may challenge candidates who experience anxiety, sensory sensitivities, or difficulties with verbal communication.

The pace and intensity of SQE preparation can create cognitive overload. Neurodiverse learners may need more time to consolidate information or process feedback – something that should be planned for, not apologised for.

Accessing reasonable adjustments

The *SRA's process for requesting reasonable adjustments* is detailed but can feel daunting. Candidates must submit recent diagnostic evidence and clear explanations of how their condition affects performance. Delays or incomplete evidence can lead to requests being rejected.

The key is *early action* – seek advice from your training provider or university disability team as soon as possible. Adjustments might include extra time, rest breaks, assistive technology, or a separate exam room. These changes are not "special treatment" but a means of ensuring fair access to demonstrate competence.

Study structure and self-management

The SQE requires self-directed preparation, often without the regular support of a tutor. For neurodiverse candidates who find organisation, focus, or time management difficult, this independence can be challenging.

Breaking study into *structured, achievable goals* helps maintain momentum. Tools such as mind maps, visual timetables, or text-to-speech software can make study more efficient. Many candidates benefit from short, focused study sessions with frequent breaks to reduce fatigue. A *study buddy* or accountability partner can also provide motivation and shared support.

Communication and confidence

SQE2 assessments, such as client interviews and advocacy tasks, can heighten anxiety for candidates who process information differently or who mask social communication differences. Preparation and practice are key. Rehearse common task types, record yourself, and develop scripts or prompts that help you stay focused under pressure. Small adjustments – such as clearer instructions or reduced environmental distractions – can make a significant difference.

Emotional fatigue and resilience

Neurodiverse candidates often experience additional emotional labour in managing expectations, masking, or navigating administrative processes. This can lead to fatigue or self-doubt. Building resilience means pacing yourself, celebrating progress, and recognising that your strengths – attention to detail, creative problem-solving, persistence – are valuable professional assets.

If you feel overwhelmed, reach out early to support networks such as *LawCare*, *Neurodiversity in Law*, or your university disability team.

Key takeaways

- Plan early for adjustments – don't leave paperwork until the last minute.
- Build structure into your study and use tools that suit your learning preferences.
- Seek formal and informal support – mentors, peers, and professional networks.
- Remember that the SQE tests competence, not conformity.
- Your neurodivergence is part of your professional identity – embrace the strengths it brings.

In short, success in the SQE is not about overcoming difference, but about recognising and working with the way your brain learns best.

With preparation, advocacy, and the right support, neurodiverse candidates can and do thrive in the legal profession.

Financing your SQE journey

Candidates need to plan in advance how they will finance their:

- SQE course and/or materials fees;
- SQE assessment fees, including having a strategy as to how they will finance any resits;
- accommodation costs whilst they study for the SQE, plus any overnight accommodation they may need near their SQE assessment venue(s); and
- travel costs both in relation to attending any SQE preparation course(s) and attending their SQE assessments.

Part-time work with full-time study

In an ideal world, we would recommend that SQE candidates who study full time focus 100% on their course and do not undertake any part-time work at all. However, we are aware that a high proportion of full-time students are doing at least some paid work alongside their studies. If you do need to work alongside a full-time course, we recommend limiting your paid working commitments to a maximum of one day per week, or you will risk trying to juggle competing priorities and not doing either particularly well.

If you need to work more hours, that's what part-time courses are for, as well as the more flexible study options!

In our experience, some students push back on this advice on the basis that, because they managed to work extensively alongside their A-levels and degrees, they expect to be able to do so again alongside a full-time SQE preparation course. Sadly, many will come to regret their decision to continue paid employment soon into their SQE studies, when they realise how much more demanding and intense preparing for the SQE can be.

TAKE A MOMENT ...

If you are concerned that you may be overcommitting in terms of your studies and paid work commitments, consider having a "Plan B," which reduces or eliminates the need to work, or better still, choose Plan B in the first place, such as combining full-time work with part-time study. Or consider deferring the start of your SQE journey until you have a stronger financial platform.

Financing your SQE course fees: Master's loan

On the assumption that you opt for an SQE preparation course (which we would recommend to most candidates), rather than simply purchasing study materials, there isn't a single "one-size-fits-all" strategy we would recommend as to how you should finance your course. That is because the variety in quality, length, and format of SQE courses is vast, which, not surprisingly, is reflected in the range of prices and the funding options which are available.

For most self-funding domestic students, ironically, one of the most accessible options is to commit to one of the more comprehensive (and expensive) types of SQE course, an SQE master's, which prepares you not only for SQE1 and SQE2, but also delivers additional specialist practice area knowledge outside the SQE curriculum. This option is accessible to most domestic students who have not previously studied for a master's, because funding is available by way of a master's loan from the Student Loans Company in excess of £13,000. In some cases, the loan will cover the full cost of a training provider's master's, but even for the more expensive providers, the shortfall becomes more manageable to afford than some cheaper options, as candidates may need to save less in advance or raise less by way of short-term loan finance.

Financing your SQE course fees: Loans for non-master's courses

Non-master's SQE preparation courses tend to have a smaller price tag, but can be harder to finance because master's funding isn't available. This means students on such courses may have to build up a larger pot of savings from earned income or borrow a larger sum on a short-term basis. High Street and specialist lenders who cater for candidates undertaking professional qualifications might be able to bridge the gap. Such loans tend to require repayment over a much shorter term and at higher rates of interest compared with the debt you accrue with the Student Loans Company. So, do your research before committing to any such short-term borrowing, and, above all, assess your ability to repay it when the lender requires.

Financing your SQE course fees: Scholarships

Most of the larger SQE training providers run a range of full-fee and partial scholarships to help candidates from all backgrounds with their course fees. Law schools wish to attract a diverse pool of talented students, and so not all their awards will be purely based on a candidate's academic background.

A common mistake made by some SQE candidates is not to bother applying for an SQE scholarship at all, because they weren't at the very top of their undergraduate cohort. You have nothing to lose other than the time it takes to draft your application. If you consider your submission carefully, you might surprise yourself and succeed, which would be a pretty good return for just a few hours' work!

Outside of SQE providers, the Law Society's Diversity Access Scheme, which is mostly funded by law firms and SQE providers, supports a limited number of candidates from socially mobile backgrounds with their course fees and work placements. If you are interested in applying, make sure you do so in the application window, which normally runs from February to mid-late March in the academic year prior to the start of your course.

Your local law society (i.e., the one run by practitioners in your area, rather than the student-led society at your university) may sponsor a limited number of candidates looking to qualify in your area. A large proportion of these have a "widening participation" agenda. Other local initiatives also exist, like the Stephen Denyer Scholarship, which is for aspiring social welfare lawyers in the north east of England.

For candidates who wish to work in social welfare law, the Social Welfare Solicitors Qualification Fund can help with SQE course and assessment fees. Candidates can also receive support from the Legal Social Mobility Fund.

The City of London Law Society is a great champion for widening participation in the profession. Indeed, it has been actively involved in some of the above schemes, so it is always worth checking its website for new initiatives which it may introduce in the future.

SQE assessment fees

Because the SQE is a centrally set assessment, candidates are required to book and pay to sit the assessments themselves. As a result, SQE assessment fees are not generally included in the cost of your SQE course fees and need to be separately budgeted for.

Our advice is to make sure that, before you start preparing for SQE1, self-funding candidates should have already saved or have a pipeline of funding secured to cover at least one SQE1 attempt. In round figures, this means saving at least £2,000. In an ideal world, we would recommend having at least a further £3,000 in the bank before you start SQE1, to also cover the cost of one SQE2 sit, particularly if you are committing to prepare for both parts of the SQE in a single course.

And beware the resit fee risk! With SQE1 pass rates for first sitters ranging from 46% to 60% in the first four years of the SQE, many conscientious, well-prepared candidates with excellent academic records are not passing first time. However confident you may be in your academic ability, don't assume that because you have never failed an exam in the past that you're guaranteed to pass the SQE. After all, future trainees at leading law firms are, overall, failing one or both parts of SQE1 at a much higher rate than their predecessors did under the LPC regime.

The bad news is that there are no SQE fee discounts for resitters, although if you pass one of the two SQE1 FLK papers, you only have to pay half the SQE1 assessment fee, so approximately £1,000 per FLK paper. Unfortunately, for SQE2, although there are 16 mini-assessments or "stations," there is no equivalent way that you can "bank" any part of the assessment. The only mark which matters is your aggregated, scaled score across all 16 stations. Consequently, to resit SQE2, you will always pay the full fee. Fortunately, the first-sitters' pass rate for SQE2 is much higher than SQE1, ranging in the first four years of the SQE from 69% to 84%, so the risk of paying for more than one SQE2 assessment fee is much lower. That said, having to find around £3,000 to resit SQE2 is a situation you don't want to find yourself in.

When it comes to booking to sit any SQE assessment, you need to be confident that you will be fully prepared and able to sit on the dates you book, because the SRA's cancellation policy is pretty strict. In particular, unless you are able to demonstrate mitigating circumstances (i.e., an intervening event which has a significant adverse effect on your performance), you will lose the whole of your exam fee if you don't attend the assessment or cancel fewer than 14 days before the start of the relevant assessment window. You will lose 75% of the fee if you cancel fewer than four weeks before the assessment (but more than 14 days before the start of the assessment window). For more details about the SRA's cancellation policy, see Part 1 "How to cancel your SQE place" (pages 46–47) and the SRA's website.

Financing your SQE assessment fees: SQE Access and Reinvestment Fund

In 2025, a limited fund of £360,000 was made available by the SRA to support candidates from disadvantaged backgrounds with their SQE assessment fees, called the *SQE Access and Reinvestment Fund.* Eleven organisations have access to the fund and all run separate schemes by which they make awards, each with different candidate selection processes.

The fund is made up of what the SRA calls "performance-based payments" paid by Kaplan, the SQE Assessment provider, and its suppliers, pursuant to their contractual obligations to deliver the SQE.

As this fund is relatively new at the time of this publication, it would be premature for us to review its impact on the individuals it benefits at this stage. However, as £360,000 will benefit only around 180 SQE1 first sitters, its initial reach will be very limited, bearing in mind we would now expect around 12,000 SQE1 first sitters across both sittings in 2026. For this initiative to have a significant long-term impact, we would like to see a regular, much larger pipeline of funding coming from those who run the SQE, which we hope the SRA will actively seek when its contract with Kaplan comes up for renewal.

Case studies of SQE journeys

Having completed this introductory chapter, you may find Case studies 1.1 to 1.6 helpful to illustrate some of the more popular qualification journeys. One or two of these may resonate with your situation.

CASE STUDY 1.1 A LINEAR JOURNEY FOR A CANDIDATE WITH A 2:2

Alexia has just graduated with a high 2:2 in her LLB. There were mitigating circumstances with Alexia's final degree award, largely because of a long illness and the subsequent death of a close family member. Alexia has been advised that one way to mitigate her degree classification would be to perform well in the SQE. Alexia has decided to commit to a comprehensive SQE LLM, largely financed by a master's student loan from Student Finance (England). The master's combines preparation for SQE1 and SQE2, plus a term focusing on additional knowledge and skills, which may give her a slight edge when applying to law firms whose practice areas align with the extra knowledge she will acquire.

Alexia will live at home with her family and will have enough saved to cover the SQE1 and SQE2 assessment fees by the time she starts her LLM. Her QWE strategy includes making use of the Law Careers Service at her SQE provider to prepare applications for roles she has a realistic prospect of securing after completing her SQE assessments and LLM.

Alexia will also commit to engaging with the training provider's Legal Advice Clinic to further develop her skill set, thereby making her more employable.

CASE STUDY 1.2 A NON-LINEAR SQE JOURNEY

Bilal has just graduated with a 2:1 in his LLB. He will self-finance his SQE journey as he does not wish to train at a law firm which sponsors its future trainees.

Although he hasn't managed to save the full amount of an integrated SQE1 and SQE2 course and the exam fees, he has enough to cover the fees for an SQE1 preparation course, his SQE1 assessment fees, and his living expenses whilst he studies and prepares for SQE1 full time over the next six months.

He wants to start his SQE journey now, whilst the FLK from his LLB is relatively fresh. If he passes SQE1, he plans to work full-time for a year in a paralegal role, during which he hopes to accrue one year's QWE. He plans to save enough over those 12 months to finance his SQE2 preparation course and assessment fees. If all goes to plan, Bilal will only have a few months' QWE to accrue by the time he receives his SQE2 results.

CASE STUDY 1.3 A PARALEGAL JOURNEY

Connie wasn't quite sure which pathway to take after she secured a 2:1 in her LLB, so she travelled for a year. On her return, she thought that working as a paralegal for a short period might help her work out whether she wanted a career in the legal profession.

She has now been working as a paralegal for nine months, has really enjoyed it and is now sure that she wants to qualify as a solicitor. Connie wants to stay in her current role, as she is getting a lot of positive feedback and is confident that the work she is currently doing will amount to QWE.

Connie has approached her firm to help support her SQE journey, as the employer of a friend in a similar position at a slightly larger firm has agreed to pay his SQE assessment fees. Unfortunately, Connie's law firm does not have the resources to sponsor candidates for the SQE. However, as the firm sees her long-term potential, they have agreed to provide an interest-free loan to cover the first sit of her SQE1 and SQE2 assessments.

Connie enjoys the sociable nature of face-to-face teaching and has opted for a part-time master's SQE preparation course, which she can finance from Student Finance (England). She will make up the small shortfall from money she has already saved in her paralegal role.

Connie may be able to qualify in around 18–24 months without changing jobs if she studies for and passes the SQE as a part-time student alongside her paralegal role over this period.

CASE STUDY 1.4 A JOURNEY OF A LAW CONVERTER WHO HAS NO FAMILY SUPPORT

Dee is financially independent of their family and needs to work alongside their SQE studies, as they did throughout their non-law degree, which they completed three years ago with first-class honours. Dee has been in a well-paid non-law graduate job for three years, from which they have saved enough to finance a PGDL. Dee wants to become a solicitor and has been advised that, with their strong academic record, they have a reasonably good prospect of securing opportunities for a sponsored QWE training contract. However, at this stage, Dee doesn't feel confident enough to apply to law firms.

Dee's law conversion and QWE strategy is to complete a part-time law conversion course as a master's with live online teaching, which will offer enough geographic flexibility around their paid work commitments, and will also help them save for the SQE if they do not secure a sponsored QWE training contract.

Dee had thought about studying full-time and continuing to work, but was worried about overcommitting. Dee's training provider's course terms and conditions stated that it was possible to transfer from the full-time to a part-time cohort in the event that their personal circumstances changed. However, continuity for Dee was more important, having been advised that a full-time student who later wants to transfer to part-time study may have to wait until an appropriate time to transfer, which might mean a delay of several months in their studies.

Like Alexia (Case study 1.1), Dee will build on their already extensive research into legal employers by consulting the Law Careers Service at their PGDL provider in order to build their confidence to make applications for a sponsored QWE training contract.

CASE STUDY 1.5 COMBINING PART-TIME STUDY ON A FLEXIBLE APP WITH PART-TIME WORK

Like a number of her peers, Erin applied for a QWE training contract in both the second and third years of her law degree. Whilst she did not secure any offers, she did manage to get through to an assessment centre at one firm and is determined to continue to apply to similar firms.

Erin is preparing for the SQE by way of a non-master's online programme. She will study on the programme for 30 hours per week. She is comfortable controlling the timing of when she studies, and so a flexible programme, which is largely self-taught, aligns with her learning preferences. Erin's working hours are not consistent enough for regular timetabled live teaching, so having such a flexible study option was important to her.

She has saved £2,000 from her part-time job towards her course fees and will continue working 20 hours per week to cover her rent and general subsistence.

Erin's online programme is not eligible for funding from Student Finance (England). Instead, she will borrow £10,000 from her bank by way of a career development loan to cover the balance needed to fund her remaining course fees and her first sits of SQE1 and SQE2. Although the interest rate is higher than SLC funding and the loan needs to be repaid in five years, Erin did not want to add to her long-term student debt.

CASE STUDY 1.6 A FULLY SPONSORED STUDENT'S JOURNEY

Felicia applied to several leading law firms for a training contract during the final two years of her law degree. She was eventually successful. Her future employer requires her to start her SQE master's at its preferred training provider starting in the September immediately after she graduates with her LLB.

Felicia's future employer will cover the full cost of the course and the fees for her first sit of each SQE assessment. In addition, she will receive a maintenance grant of £15,000 from the firm, which will cover her rent and subsistence during her SQE studies.

Ultimately, the firm reserves the right to release Felicia from her training contract should she fail any SQE assessment. The terms and conditions of the firm's training contract offer don't commit to paying for resit fees in the event that Felicia fails any SQE assessment: the firm says it will deal with any such candidate on a case-by-case basis. Felicia is aware that some previous candidates at the same firm (but not all) lost their training contract after failing an SQE assessment, so it is particularly important to her that she passes all her SQE exams first time.

2

SQE1

The SQE1 assessments

There is no doubt that the SQE1 assessments are challenging. Candidates sit two papers, each of which contains 180 multiple-choice questions and lasts for five hours and six minutes. The SQE1 assessments test candidates' "Functioning Legal Knowledge": this is the knowledge the SRA requires you to have to be able to qualify as a solicitor. It is often referred to simply as the "FLK."

An important thing to understand about FLK is that it entails both 1) underlying law subjects that you will typically study during an undergraduate law degree or law conversion course and 2) a series of foundational legal practice subjects.

This is a summary of the FLK covered in each of the two SQE1 papers:

- Paper 1 (FLK1): Business Law and Practice, Dispute Resolution, Contract, Tort, the Legal System of England and Wales, Constitutional and Administrative Law and EU Law, Legal Services, and Ethics and Professional Conduct.
- Paper 2 (FLK2): Property Practice, Wills and the Administration of Estates, Solicitors Accounts, Land law, Trusts, Criminal Law, Criminal Law and Practice, and Ethics and Professional Conduct.

When you sit each paper, you will be required to answer a significant number of multiple-choice questions (MCQs) in each of the subjects covered by that paper. The questions are randomised, which means that you must be comfortable jumping between the different subjects. So you might encounter a tort question, then two dispute resolution questions, then an ethics and professional conduct question, and so on. This highlights the importance of having a really firm grip on all of the

DOI: 10.4324/9781003639671-3

FLK by the time you sit the SQE1 assessments, so that you can move between subjects with ease.

Each SQE1 paper is split into two parts: this means that the total length of each paper is five hours and six minutes, with each part lasting two hours and 33 minutes. You will sit the first part, have a one-hour break, and then sit the second part. Each part contains different questions, and you will not be able to revisit questions from the first part after it has ended. You are permitted to access your personal belongings and leave the assessment centre during the one-hour break.

Across the whole of each FLK paper, you will have 180 single best answer multiple-choice questions (SBA MCQs) to answer. If you divide the total available time by the number of questions, this comes to an average of one minute and 42 seconds per question. The assessment platform allows you to flag questions you would like to revisit. The nature of MCQs means that, even if you do not know the answer to a question, you should nominate an answer before moving on: there is no concept of negative marking in the SQE.

Although each SQE1 assessment day can be a gruelling experience, well-prepared candidates do have enough time to answer all of the questions.

The SRA has published the assessment specification for SQE1, available on the SRA's SQE website, and sets out the FLK to be assessed. The SRA emphasises the importance of candidates understanding fundamental legal principles rather than, for example, the precise statutory citation or case name relevant to a particular question. The exception to this is where the section number or case name has been adopted as the name of a legal principle in its own right, e.g., Rylands v Fletcher or a Part 36 Offer. This means that, as a general rule, you do not need to know case names or individual statutory references, but occasionally this is necessary.

The cut-off date for examinable law is four months prior to the date of the first assessment in the relevant SQE1 assessment window. For the avoidance of doubt, this date is confirmed on the assessment dates and booking windows page of the SRA's SQE website.

You have six years from the date of your first attempt at SQE1 to pass both SQE1 and SQE2, and you have a maximum of three attempts at each paper within this window. At the time of publication, you must sit both papers in the same sitting (unless you have already passed one, in which case you only need to sit the outstanding paper). Note that this is different from SQE2, which is an "all or nothing" assessment: if you do not pass SQE2, you must resit all aspects of the assessment.

The pass mark for each SQE1 paper is determined by the SRA/Kaplan as part of their post-assessment process. To ensure fairness between students who have sat different papers during the same sitting, the SRA/Kaplan employs a system of "scaled scoring."

In your results, the SRA/Kaplan tells you whether your mark is "pass" or "not pass," and which quintile your mark falls into. A quintile is a "slice" of 20% of the candidates who sat the paper, ranked in order of how they performed. So, a person whose mark fell into the first quintile was among the top 20% of candidates for the paper. For further details on the marking process for SQE1, including scaled scoring, please see "Results and marking" (pages 54–57).

The SQE assessments may be undertaken in English or Welsh.

You can access sample SQE1 questions on the SRA's SQE website.

SBA MCQs

The MCQs that you will encounter in SQE1 are "single best answer" multiple-choice questions. The aim of each question is to require you to analyse a set of client facts and apply your understanding of the FLK by providing the most appropriate advice to your client. Attention to detail (a very important skill for solicitors in practice) is essential for success in the SQE1 assessments.

Each MCQ is structured in the same way: it starts with a fact pattern/scenario which explains who the client is and what has happened. It then asks the question and gives you five plausible options to choose from. A crucial aspect of SBA MCQs is that more than one option may, technically, be correct; the crucial thing is that one option is objectively best. It is often the case that you can determine what the best answer will be before reading through the options included with the question. It is essential, however, to carefully read all the options, some of which can be very similar, before deciding which one to select.

Tips for answering SBA MCQs

- Answer the question in front of you. Do not infer facts or answer a similar but not identical question (perhaps because you have encountered a similar question during your preparation).
- Take time to read the question carefully. Do not be tempted to skim-read and rush. Reading the question carefully gives you the best chance of answering it correctly the first time: this is the most efficient way to get through the paper.

- Take a moment to think what the answer might be before you read the options. If the answer you think of is one of the options, this will give you a head start in answering the question.
- Read the options carefully and eliminate those you know are incorrect. Then work through again and determine which is the *best* answer of the remaining options.
- If you do not know the answer, select the most plausible option, flag the question for revisiting (if you have time), and move on. If you give no answer, you will score zero for that question. Even if you have to completely guess five questions, the odds are that you will get one right! The worst-case scenario is that you are wrong and get zero, but if you don't select any answer for any of the five MCQs, you'll get zero anyway.
- Be conscious of the average time allocation of one minute 42 seconds per question. This is longer than you think. You will need more time than this for some questions and less for others. Make time during your preparation to practise SQE1 assessment-level MCQs under timed conditions so that you have a good idea of how long you have per question.
- If you have time at the end of the assessment, revisit the questions you have flagged.
- Sometimes unpacking the facts of a complex scenario by way of a diagram can give clarity to what's going on, especially if you are a visual learner. See how in Figure 2.1, we have unpacked the facts of the scenario on the left into a simple diagram on the right.

Example MCQ scenario:

A pension company granted a 10 year commercial lease of a retail unit in 2017 to a hairdresser.

The hairdresser subsequently assigned the lease to a hardware store. The hardware store assigned the lease to a florist. The florist assigned the lease to a grocer. All the assignments were made with the landlord's consent.

For all three assignments, the pension company required an authorised guarantee agreement from the outgoing tenant.

The Grocer has failed to pay the latest quarter's rent.

Apart from the Grocer, from whom can the pension company recover the outstanding rent?

[Options not shown for the purpose of this example]

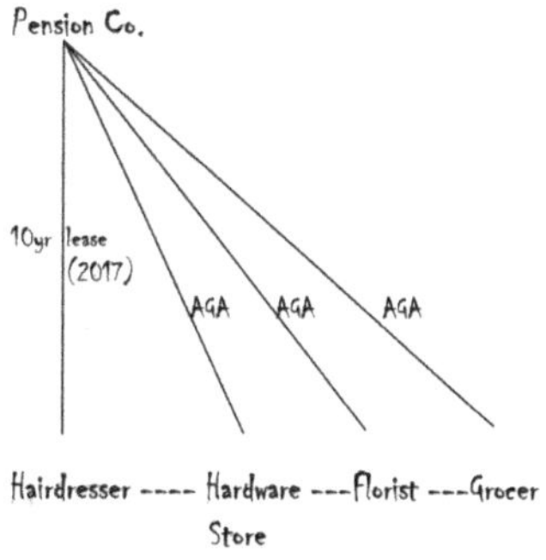

FIGURE 2.1 An example of how to unpack a complex fact pattern.

SQE preparation, planning, and common pitfalls

Do not underestimate the challenge

The broad nature of the FLK assessed in SQE1 means that it is likely that you will need to retain more information for the SQE1 assessments than for any other assessment you have attempted. Do not underestimate this challenge. It will be important for you to commit sufficient time to revise all of the subjects that are assessed, including the time which will be required to update subjects you may have studied a number of years ago.

Make sure you have consistently practised assessment-style questions using good-quality sample MCQs. Do not, however, rely on attempting MCQs as a substitute for undertaking deep learning of the legal material being assessed. A combination of learning the FLK thoroughly and having practised good-quality MCQs in exam conditions will prepare you well for the assessments.

Do sweat the small stuff: Details matter!

The way in which SBA MCQs are drafted means that there will often be only a small difference between the options available. It is possible that, for a given question, more than one of the options will be, technically, correct: your task is to identify which of the options is the *best* answer. This highlights the importance of reading all five options carefully and calmly before making your choice.

There are two common mistakes people make when answering SBA MCQs. The first is to skim-read the options too quickly, which means they do not notice the subtleties in the drafting, leading them to opt for the first option that appears right, rather than reading to the end and finding a "better" option. The second is that they encounter a question that is similar to others they have attempted in that subject area, and they then make assumptions about the facts and/or what the question is asking. Although you will be time-limited in the assessment, there is no substitute for reading the whole question before selecting your answer. As soon as you are confident you have given the best answer you can, move on to the next question.

Leave yourself time

In each half of each SQE1 assessment, there will be 90 questions to attempt within two hours and 33 minutes. This means that you will have one minute and 42 seconds per question. Some questions will feel quite straightforward, and you will be able to answer them in less than one minute and 42 seconds; others may take longer than that to attempt. As such, you may find it helpful to think of this in a different way, for example, that you have just over ten minutes to attempt every six questions.

Practising assessment-standard MCQs in exam conditions (including exam timings) will help you to calibrate how long you have per question. Remember that you can flag a question and return to it at the end of the assessment to review your work. If you are unsure but feel you have spent enough time on that question, give your best answer and then come back to it at the end if you have time.

Are you ready?

The cost of the SQE1 assessments and the fact that you have only three attempts to pass SQE1 mean that you should not book to sit until you are confident that you will be ready. There is, of course, a balance to be struck as booking for SQE1 tends to take place about four months in advance of the assessments themselves.

As the booking date approaches, you should carefully and honestly analyse what you have done and what remains outstanding. Take into account the fact that, if you are undertaking a course to study some or all of the material, sitting the assessment at the first available sitting after you have completed those studies is likely to optimise your SQE performance, as at least some of the material will be fresh in your mind. It is also important to acknowledge that the broad nature of the SQE1 specification means that almost nobody ever feels completely ready.

The SRA places the responsibility on candidates to sit the SQE assessments only if they are fit to do so. For this purpose, being fit to sit means that you do not know of any reason why your performance would be adversely affected during the assessment or why you may subsequently bring a claim for mitigating circumstances. Examples of situations which may impair a candidate's fitness to sit include their own illness, the illness of a close relative, or a bereavement. At the beginning of each SQE assessment, you will be required to declare that you are fit to sit. If you are not fit to sit, you should *not* give this declaration, and you should not sit the assessment.

Booking the SQE1 assessments

The booking procedure for SQE1 has evolved since the SQE was introduced and is likely to continue to evolve. The information in this section refers to the regime in place when this book went to press, but you should always check the SRA's SQE website for the most up-to-date details and requirements.

The first step in the booking process is to register for the SQE by creating a candidate account at the SRA's SQE website. You will need to activate your account, then log in and verify your identity using a government-issued photo identity document. You only need to do this once.

The second step of the process must be undertaken for each SQE assessment you book. You are required to complete a series of pre-booking steps, including:

- completing a diversity survey;
- confirming any exemptions you may have (this is only relevant to candidates who already have legal qualifications that might exempt them from aspects of the SQE); and
- confirming whether or not you wish to request reasonable adjustments to sit the assessment you are planning to book. Note that it is essential that you agree on any reasonable adjustments with the SRA as early as you can (see "Requesting reasonable adjustments for SQE assessments" (pages 44–45)).

The third step of the process for all candidates is to complete a seat reservation form. A link to this form is sent by email to all candidates who are registered to sit SQE1 approximately four months in advance of the assessments. The date and time for the form's circulation will be published in advance by the SRA. You should diarise this date and time and submit your form as soon as you are able on that day. This is because the forms are processed and places are allocated on a first-come, first-served basis, and you only have a short time to complete the form (usually three business days).

The form asks you to provide information including:

- your SQE candidate number;
- whether you require a reasonable adjustment;
- your preferred assessment venue; and
- your preferred assessment dates.

TAKE A MOMENT...

Think strategically as to which day of the week you want to sit FLK1 in the first week and FLK2 in the following week. You don't have to sit them exactly a week apart. In fact, given that students report revising more for

FLK1 (as it is their first paper) and find FLK2 a little more challenging, why not book FLK1 on the Monday or Tuesday of week one and FLK2 on the Thursday or Friday of the following week? That way, you can maximise your revision time between the two papers.

In the fourth step of the process, the SRA will inform you of the SQE venues and dates you have been allocated. This happens around four weeks after the booking window first opens. In order to accept your place, you must log into your account on the SRA's SQE website and make payment (or, if you are a reasonable adjustments student, you should follow the SRA's instructions for making payment). It is important to take account of the deadline by which you must pay for your place, as it is generally very short (usually two business days). You are not obliged to accept your allocated place: it is open to you to decline (or simply not confirm) your allocated place, in which case it will be reallocated to another candidate.

TAKE A MOMENT ...

If your decision is borderline as to whether you think you will be ready to sit the assessment, you should still complete the booking form when the booking window opens because you only commit to sitting the assessment if you pay the fee, when requested, a few weeks later.

At the end of the booking period, there is generally a relatively short period of time (usually one week) during which candidates can seek to change the location or date of their booking, or, if they did not submit a seat reservation form, make a booking, subject to availability.

To give more insight into the process, Figure 2.2 shows the key dates in the booking window for candidates who booked to sit SQE1 in

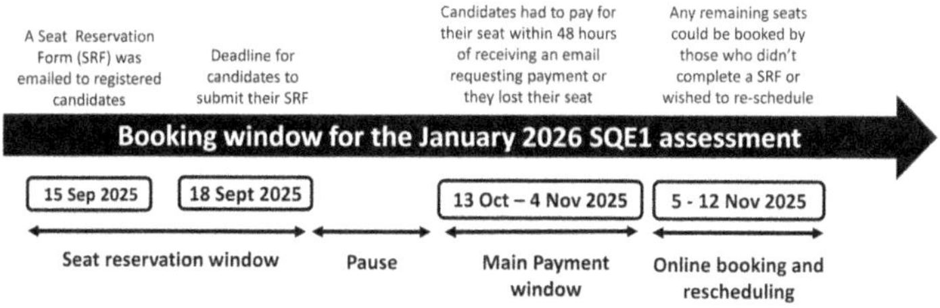

FIGURE 2.2 Booking window: January 2026 SQE1 assessment.

January 2026. Figure 2.2 is provided for illustrative purposes only: you should always check the up-to-date booking rules and timings for each SQE assessment on the SRA's SQE website.

Requesting reasonable adjustments for SQE assessments

If you wish to request reasonable adjustments for any SQE assessment, you should register for your SQE account and complete the reasonable adjustments application as early as you can.

Under the SRA's Reasonable Adjustments policy, which applies from October 2026, reasonable adjustments must be agreed by the deadline to submit a seat reservation form for the exam sit in question. This is very early in the process and means that reasonable adjustments candidates must turn their attention to this process well in advance of bookings opening.

A reasonable adjustment liaison from Kaplan will then work with you to agree on the reasonable adjustments to which you are entitled. It is at the discretion of Kaplan whether you are entitled to reasonable adjustments and, if so, what they should be. The SQE Reasonable Adjustments policy and SQE reasonable adjustments FAQs are available on the SRA's SQE website.

To be granted reasonable adjustments, you will be required to provide supporting evidence from a doctor or other appropriate professional that explains:

- the nature of your disability or condition;
- the substantial disadvantage you will have without adjustments; and
- details of the adjustments made in your workplace and/or with your training provider, where relevant.

TAKE A MOMENT ...

Because the range of SQE assessments is so varied, especially for SQE2, it is really important that candidates applying for reasonable adjustments ensure that the medical expert(s) writing their report(s) fully understand the nature and length of each SQE assessment and how the candidate's disability or condition is affected. Ideally, they should suggest what they, in their professional opinion, would recommend as the reasonable

> adjustment(s) for each part of each assessment. Whilst such recommendations will not be binding on Kaplan (because they need to ensure there is consistency in the adjustments offered to similarly affected candidates), there is a much greater prospect of a candidate being offered something close to (if not precisely) what the report recommends than leaving it to Kaplan's discretion.

It is crucial that you provide all supporting evidence that Kaplan requests in respect of your application for reasonable adjustments as early in the process as you can. Similarly, you should promptly provide any requested additional information and respond to confirm whether you accept their proposed adjustments. This allows for the reasonable adjustments process to be completed by the deadline for submitting a seat reservation form. If reasonable adjustments are not agreed by that time, you may not be able to sit the assessments in that assessment window with the adjustments you need.

Examples of reasonable adjustments which may be put in place for SQE assessments include:

- extra time for candidates with dyslexia or other specific learning or cognitive conditions;
- additional/extended breaks for candidates who have conditions giving rise to fatigue; or
- a separate room (or a room shared with only a few other candidates).

Note that it is not possible to receive reasonable adjustments to take account of the fact that you are not sitting the assessment in your first language.

Your Reasonable Adjustment Liaison will make a proposal of reasonable adjustments. You can either accept this proposal or decline it (in which case, it may be possible to agree to alternative adjustments). Once your reasonable adjustments have been agreed, you can submit a seat reservation form.

Note that it may not be possible to receive your reasonable adjustments at the assessment centres closest to your home; you may need to travel to a more distant location in order to receive your agreed adjustments.

You can track the status of your reasonable adjustments application via your SQE account on the SRA's SQE website.

Fees

At the time of writing, the fee to sit SQE1 is £2,006 (made up of £1,003 for FLK1 and £1,003 for FLK2). Fees tend to increase each September, and it is important you check the current fees on the SRA SQE website. You must pay the applicable booking fee in full at the time that you confirm your acceptance of the SQE1 seat(s) you have been allocated. There are two ways to pay SQE fees:

- The first is to pay by debit or credit card: all major card types are accepted, including American Express.
- The second is to redeem a prepaid voucher purchased by your training provider or employer. This method is less commonly used; examples include where vouchers are purchased by apprenticeship employers or by some law schools on behalf of sponsored students. To redeem the voucher, you enter a unique code when making payment.

If you need to resit one or both of the SQE1 assessments, you must pay the full fee again for the paper(s) you need to resit. This means that if you need to resit only one paper, you only pay for that paper.

How to cancel your SQE place

If you have booked to sit SQE1 or SQE2 but decide that you cannot sit after all, you should cancel your place as soon as possible. You will likely incur a substantial cancellation fee (unless you are able to claim mitigating circumstances – see below), but it will mean that you maintain your three attempts at each of SQE1 and SQE2, even if you were not able to sit.

You can cancel your place for either SQE1 or SQE2 by submitting the Model Cancellation Form contained in Schedule 1 of the SRA's SQE Assessment Terms and Conditions published on the SRA's SQE website. Note that the form provides wording which you must email or post to the SRA (details included in the form).

When deciding whether to cancel a booking, it is important to carefully consult the SRA Assessment Terms and Conditions to understand the level of cancellation fee you will incur. As a general rule, the later you cancel, the greater the cancellation fee will be. For example, if you cancel more than four weeks before the assessment window starts, you will likely be charged a cancellation fee of 25% of the assessment fee; after that, the cancellation fee increases significantly.

TAKE A MOMENT ...

If you book and pay for an SQE assessment and subsequently believe you may not be able to sit, it is important to cancel at the earliest possible opportunity because the cancellation charges rack up very quickly. There is a 14-day cooling-off period after booking during which candidates can cancel and receive a full refund. After that, the cancellation charges are:

- 25% of the assessment fee if you cancel after the end of the booking window but over four weeks before the start of the assessment window;
- after that, 75% of the assessment fee is retained as a cancellation charge, unless you cancel less than 96 hours before the start of the assessment window; and
- no refund will be claimable unless you make a successful mitigating circumstances application if you cancel less than 96 hours before the assessment or simply do not sit.

Note that there is no concept of deferring a booking for the SQE1 centralised assessments: you must, instead, cancel and rebook for a later sit.

Depending on your reason for not being able to sit, you may be able to claim mitigating circumstances (see below).

The practicalities: Before, during, and after the exam

Timelines

At the time of writing, there were two opportunities to sit SQE1 each year: the first in January and the second in July. It is possible that the SRA will introduce additional SQE1 sits in the future.

If you find out that you have not passed SQE1, it is important that you check the timings for booking the next sit so that, if you would like to resit immediately, you do not miss the booking window. There is generally a period of two to four weeks between the release of results for one SQE1 sit and the opening of the booking window for the next sit. There is no obligation to resit immediately, so you should think carefully about factors that may affect your likelihood of success in a resit and what you need to have done in order to be ready for it before you commit to booking again.

Security screening procedures

In addition to the standard security checks when you arrive at the test centre (referred to below), some test venues employ security wanding as a further security measure. This is a non-contact procedure under which you are first scanned (over your clothing) with an infrared wand; if the infrared wand triggers an alert, you are scanned by a metal detection wand. If both wands are triggered, you may be refused entry to the exam room. If you have a medical item that may set off the wands, you must declare it in advance via the reasonable adjustments process. If you wear a medical device which could be adversely affected by the wanding process (such as a pacemaker), you may apply for a formal wanding exemption before the assessment day via the reasonable adjustments process. If you need to carry or wear a metal or magnetic item for religious purposes (such as a Kirpan or magnetic fastenings on religious headwear) you must contact the SRA's candidate services team to declare this in advance. Note that the deadline to submit all medical or religious declarations or exemption requests is the date on which bookings close for the particular sit of the SQE1 assessments.

What to expect on the day

The SQE1 assessments are conducted under strict, closed-book exam conditions in Pearson Vue test centres. These are distributed throughout the UK and in some countries overseas. You will sit the assessments on a computer provided by the venue and will have a small, erasable whiteboard to use as a notepad and marker pen to make notes. You may not take anything else into the exam room, such as mobile phones, watches, food, or a drink. The assessment platform provides a calculator. You are permitted to leave the room for a comfort break or to eat, drink, or take medication, but note that the assessment clock will continue during that time. You are not permitted to leave the assessments early.

At your Pearson Vue test centre, there are likely to be candidates sitting a wide range of different assessments, many of which are shorter than the SQE1 assessments. You should expect there to be other candidates coming and going, so it is important to be mentally prepared and try not to let it put you off or cause you to lose concentration.

You will have received a personalised email from Kaplan that gives clear assessment day instructions, including the address of your SQE1 test centre and the time you should arrive. You will also be notified of the assessment start time and the length of the assessment day. Note that SQE1 assessments start at different times of day, so it is essential to check your own information and not to rely on information received by any other candidate. You should take particular care if you are sitting in a different time zone from those sitting in the UK.

It is essential that you arrive at the relevant Pearson Vue test centre in good time. If you are late, you will not be allowed to sit the assessment. Plan your travel in advance and, if possible, undertake a trial run of the journey at a similar time of day. You should also have a backup plan in case of travel issues, such as a cancelled train or a traffic jam. Remember that some venues are very large, so it is important to have established certain essential practical details in advance, such as which entrance to use. Some candidates find that they need to stay overnight near the venue because they cannot be sure they will arrive on time on the morning of the assessment.

Whilst there is space at the Pearson Vue test centres to store small bags, you are not permitted to take large bags/luggage. If you cannot avoid having a large bag with you, you should make a plan for storing it elsewhere, for example, in a station's left-luggage locker. Plan how you will deal with your belongings in advance: do not leave it to chance.

When you arrive at the test centre, you will register and complete a series of identity and security checks. The SRA recommends you take your current, valid passport as a primary form of identification, supported by a second form of ID that contains your full name and signature (e.g., a signed debit or credit card). Take careful account of the information on the required identity documents contained in your confirmation email; the SRA's requirements may evolve over time.

Students who have sat SQE assessments report being subjected to a range of personal inspections before entering the assessment room: for example, be prepared to be asked to roll up your sleeves, to pull up your hair to show that you are not wearing any hidden devices, and for any spectacles you wear to be inspected.

Once you are in the assessment room, you will sit at a computer and be asked to provide a series of confirmations. First, that you are fit to sit the assessment. This means that you will be confirming that you know of no reason why your assessment performance would be adversely affected or why you may subsequently feel the need to bring a claim for mitigating circumstances. Examples of factors which might render you unfit to sit the assessment include your own illness or the illness of a close family member. If you are not fit to sit, you should *not* give the fit to sit declaration, and you should withdraw from sitting the assessment. Note that it is unlikely that you will be able to recover your booking fee if you sign the declaration and commence the assessment but subsequently withdraw.

The next confirmation you will give is that you have read, understood, and agree to be bound by the SRA Candidate Confidentiality Policy. It is important for you to have read and checked your understanding of this policy in advance. The essence of this policy is that you understand that the content of the assessment is confidential and that you will not disclose or discuss its content with any other person.

Finally, you must confirm that you agree to be bound by the SQE Assessment Regulations. Again, it is important to have read and checked that you understand the meaning of these regulations in advance of the assessment.

The total exam time for each paper is five hours and six minutes, split into two sessions of two hours and 33 minutes. The break between the two sessions is approximately one hour long. You must register for the second session at least ten minutes before it starts, so you should plan on taking a break of no more than 40–45 minutes.

Tips for getting the best out of the exam day

- Practise MCQs under exam conditions to help you understand how you will respond to sitting in the assessment centre. This should include attempting a set of MCQs under timed conditions, ideally on an unfamiliar computer and without making any reference to your notes.
- Get a good night's sleep! SQE1 is like no other exam you will have previously sat. It requires mental agility throughout the whole day. A late or all-night last-minute revision session will have a negative impact on your stamina for the assessment day. The last thing you want to do is risk mental fatigue, which seriously compromises your sleep pattern.
- Have as clear an idea in your head as you can of what the assessment day will be like in advance. Mentally prepare yourself for each part, as explained above.
- Have a trial run of your journey to the venue and check you know where you will need to go.
- Eat a good breakfast and bring enough food and drink to keep you going, as you may not have time to purchase additional food locally.
- Arrive in good time.
- Bring your identity documents and any medication you need.
- Dress comfortably, including layers, so that you can adjust to the temperature of the exam room.

- Make good use of the break between the two sessions. Rehydrate and eat food that will give you energy for the second session. Decompress by, for example, undertaking breathing exercises or going for a walk in the fresh air.
- Once each session has finished, try not to dwell on the questions/ the answers you have given.

After the assessment: What happens next?

After you have sat the two SQE1 assessment papers, allow yourself some time to relax and decompress. For all candidates, the assessments are genuinely challenging, and it is important to allow yourself the time and opportunity to recharge.

What if something goes wrong during the assessment?

Mitigating circumstances

What if you fall ill during the assessment?

If you become unwell during your SQE assessment and are not able to continue, you should inform an invigilator immediately. You should then contact the SRA immediately after the assessment to discuss making an application for mitigating circumstances (see below).

What if you are disturbed by external factors such as noise or illness?

The SRA notes on its SQE website that the test centres are located in city centres and that they do not have control over building or traffic noise that may occur outside. If you feel that external noise or disruptions have disturbed your assessment or you are unwell to such a degree that your performance has been materially and adversely affected, you may want to consider applying for mitigating circumstances. Make sure your complaint/ illness is fully recorded by an invigilator before you leave the assessment venue, who should give you a case reference number at the venue on the day, as you will need to refer to it in your mitigating circumstances application.

How to apply for mitigating circumstances

The SRA's policy on mitigating circumstances is set out on the SRA's SQE website.

There are three categories of mitigating circumstances available for the SQE assessments:

- a mistake or irregularity in the administration or conduct of the assessment;
- evidence of bias in the conduct of the assessment; or
- a candidate's illness or other personal circumstances beyond their reasonable control.

In each case, the circumstances must have, or be likely to have, materially and adversely affected the candidate's marks or performance in the assessment.

If you believe that you can demonstrate mitigating circumstances, you may be able to make a claim. Note that it may be possible to claim mitigating circumstances if you did not sit a particular SQE assessment for one of the reasons outlined above. However, it is not possible to claim mitigating circumstances if you failed to attend both SQE1 papers or all SQE2 assessment stations. For this reason, it is important to cancel your place at the earliest opportunity if you know that you will not be able to sit any aspect of the SQE1 or SQE2 assessments you have booked because mitigating circumstances will not be available.

If you declared yourself fit to sit at the start of your SQE assessment, it is very unlikely that you will be granted mitigating circumstances. This is why you should think carefully before making your fit to sit confirmation.

If you decide to make a claim for mitigating circumstances, you must complete the relevant Mitigating Circumstances form via the SRA's SQE portal. You must attach independent supporting written evidence of your mitigating circumstances. If these relate to illness, you must attach a medical certificate that provides evidence of your illness, including relevant dates and the nature, onset, and duration of the condition. If they relate to a bereavement, you will be expected to provide evidence such as a death certificate, proof of relationship, and evidence of the effect on you (e.g., medical evidence).

We recommend that you apply for mitigating circumstances as soon as you can after the assessment, if necessary. The deadline for SQE1 assessments is 16:00 UK local time on the fifth working day after the relevant booked assessment. Note that you should make your own individual mitigating circumstances application, even if you know that the issue affects multiple other candidates who are also planning to apply for mitigating circumstances.

If your claim for mitigating circumstances is accepted, the SRA will usually discount the assessment in respect of which you made your claim. This means it will not be counted as one of your three attempts to sit SQE1. In this case, you can expect to be refunded 75% of the cost of the relevant assessment. Note that your SQE1 mark cannot be changed as a result of a mitigating circumstances finding.

If your claim for mitigating circumstances is unsuccessful, your SQE1 result will stand and will be recorded as one of your attempts on your candidate account.

Assessment delivery disruption

An assessment delivery disruption (or ADD) is a formal status declared by Kaplan where a system, technical, or other operational failure prevents an SQE assessment from starting or being completed on a particular day. If the issue cannot be resolved within a reasonable time, Kaplan will declare an ADD, and you will be asked to leave the test centre. It is relatively unusual for this to occur. Examples of events which have previously caused assessment delivery failure include power cuts and IT problems affecting the relevant assessment centre.

Kaplan will prioritise rescheduling the assessment as soon as possible, ideally within two to three days of your original date.

If you have not attempted any part of the assessment

If the ADD prevents you from starting your assessment, you will have the option of sitting the rescheduled assessment (provided you are available and happy to declare yourself fit to sit). If you are not available and fit to sit the rescheduled assessment, the assessment will be cancelled, your attempt discounted, and you will receive a refund of your assessment fees for that paper.

Note that, if the ADD prevents you from starting your FLK1 paper, you must proceed to sit FLK2. If the ADD prevents you from starting your FLK2 paper, your mark from your FLK1 paper will stand.

If you have attempted part of the assessment

If you have already started your assessment when the ADD is declared, your options are as outlined above for rescheduling the paper and/or discounting the attempt. In addition, depending on the circumstances of the ADD, there may be the option of having your assessment marked: if you pass, the mark will stand; if you fail, the attempt will be discounted, and you will receive a refund of your assessment fee for the paper.

Results and marking

How are SQE1 papers benchmarked?

Before you sit the SQE assessments, you will already know when your results will be published. For SQE1, this is usually five to six weeks after the assessments, with the outcome of mitigating circumstances applications following a little later.

Results are posted to each candidate's SRA SQE account and can be downloaded as a pdf. You will receive an email notifying you that the results are available to view.

For each of the 180 MCQs in each of the SQE1 papers, one mark will be awarded if you select the best answer of the five available options.

There is no standard pass mark for SQE1: instead, the pass mark for each paper is determined by the Assessment Board for each assessment.

An important aspect of this process is the Modified Angoff method of standard setting. Under this method, a panel of qualified solicitors determines how difficult a particular question was by considering how many out of ten "just competent" day one solicitors would have answered it correctly. Although integral to the overall process, a Modified Angoff exercise is not necessarily undertaken for every SQE1 paper. Instead, statistical equating is used to ensure consistency.

Statistical equating allows the Assessment Board to compare the difficulty of different papers by considering how candidates have performed on common questions (i.e., questions that have been repeated between papers). Having considered how candidates have performed on the common questions, the Assessment Board can look at their relative performance on the rest of the questions in each assessment in order to determine the level of difficulty (and, therefore, the appropriate pass mark) for each assessment.

The Assessment Board then considers whether any adjustment must be made for measurement error (which is a statistical adjustment that reflects the range of scores a particular candidate might achieve depending on a range of variables).

Once all adjustments have been made, the resulting mark is rounded to the nearest whole number: this is the pass mark for the assessment. If you scored this or above, you have passed the assessment.

Scaled scoring

There is one further step taken with respect to candidates' scores before they are published. All candidates' scores are placed on a scale between 0 and 500. The pass mark on that scale is always 300. Scaling scores in this way means that the results of candidates who have sat different papers can be directly compared. If you have scored exactly the pass mark in the FLK paper you sat, which might be 110/180, your scaled mark will translate as 300.

Scaling allows comparison between candidates' attempts, taking account of the fact that one paper may be slightly easier or more difficult than another. For example, a raw score of 110/180 for Paper A could be scaled as 320/500 (PASS), whilst the same raw score of 110/180 for Paper B could be scaled as 295/500 (NOT PASS). This scaling reflects the fact that Paper A is more difficult than Paper B.

CASE STUDY 2.1

In Harjan's FLK1 paper, he answered 105/180 MCQs correctly.

Iris sits a different FLK1 paper on a different day in the same SQE sit and also answered 105/180 MCQs correctly.

The examiners' analysis has shown that Harjan's paper was slightly more difficult than Iris's, and, as a consequence, they scaled Harjan's mark to 305/500 (a pass), whereas Iris's scaled mark ended up as 295/500 (a narrow fail).

So, it is possible for two students sitting separate papers to answer the same number of questions correctly, but one ends up passing and the other failing.

What is included in your results?

When you receive your SQE1 results, the key information you will see for each paper is:

- whether your result is a pass or not;
- your raw score, i.e., the number of questions you answered correctly out of 180;
- your scaled score out of 500 (with 300 being the pass mark); and
- your quintile.

Quintiles are calculated by dividing the results for all candidates who sat SQE1 in a particular sit into five equal groups based on their performance. The first (top) quintile contains the candidates with the top 20% of marks; the second quintile contains the candidates who received the next 20% of marks, and so on.

Other information that will be included in your results includes:

- the date of the relevant assessment;
- the date of the transcript (i.e., the date of the results release);
- the attempt number (remembering that you have three attempts at SQE1);
- your deadline to pass the SQE (counted as six years from the date of your first attempt at an SQE assessment); and
- a breakdown of your performance in each of the FLK subjects covered in that paper, expressed as a scaled score out of 500.

This breakdown is particularly helpful for candidates who have not passed the assessment, as it allows them to understand the FLK subjects in which they received fewer marks and where they would benefit from additional study for any resit.

If you have not passed both SQE1 assessments, you must resit any assessment you have failed before you can book SQE2.

Results where you have applied for mitigating circumstances for SQE1

All candidates who have sat SQE1 receive their results on the same day, whether or not they have applied for mitigating circumstances.

If you applied for mitigating circumstances but have passed SQE1, your mitigating circumstances claim will automatically be rejected as the SRA concludes that the circumstances behind your claim cannot have materially and adversely affected your marks or performance. Note that this means that a strong candidate who applies for mitigating circumstances but passes the assessment will have the advantage that they do not need to resit the paper, but that their score may fall into a lower quintile than they would have expected in the absence of the mitigating circumstances.

If you applied for mitigating circumstances but have not passed SQE1, you will be notified of your result on results day, but must then wait for the outcome of your mitigating circumstances claim. The date for the decision on your mitigating circumstances claim will have been communicated to you shortly after you made your application for mitigating circumstances. Usually, you will receive the outcome of your mitigating circumstances claim two to three weeks after the results publication date. If the booking window for the next sit of SQE1 is open whilst you are waiting for the outcome of your mitigating circumstances claim, you may make a booking to resit SQE1 in the next assessment window at no cost and with no obligation, pending the outcome of your claim.

Failing one or both SQE1 papers

If you sit and fail one or both SQE1 assessments, you should reflect carefully on the reasons for this. Were you adequately prepared? Was there an issue on the day that meant that you felt you were not able to give your best performance? Were there particular subjects in which you were less able to do yourself justice? Take time to analyse the subject breakdown you received with your results to help you understand where you should focus additional study in the future. Having undertaken this reflection, you should make a plan for how and when you will resit SQE1. Do you need to undertake further study? Did you allow yourself sufficient time and space to prepare the first time around? Are there things that you should change in your approach to preparation for a resit? Note that you have a total of six years from your first SQE assessment to pass both SQE1 and SQE2.

Tips for absorbing and recalling significant amounts of information

The SQE is a closed-book examination – you cannot take notes into the exam room, and you will not be able to look anything up during the assessment. On top of this, it is time pressured. That means you must be able to recall information quickly and accurately, as well as understand it sufficiently deeply to apply it to practical legal scenarios.

For many candidates, the challenge is not simply the breadth of the syllabus but the fact that they have not had to learn, retain, and recall such a large body of information for an exam in many years. If you are returning to study after a long break, or if your undergraduate degree did not involve heavy factual recall, this may feel particularly daunting.

The good news is that cognitive science offers strong evidence on how people learn and remember, and by drawing on this evidence, you can approach your SQE preparation more strategically. Understanding *how* you learn is just as important as *what* you learn.

Deep and surface learning

In educational theory, a useful distinction is made between surface learning and deep learning. Both have their place in SQE preparation, but understanding the difference will help you avoid common mistakes.

Surface learning

Surface learning is essentially about memorising facts without much understanding. For example, memorising that the limitation period for breach of contract claims is six years is a surface fact. Surface learning is useful for short-term recall of discrete points of law, procedural rules, or definitions – and there is no escaping the need for this in the SQE. Some exam questions will require nothing more than fast factual recall.

However, surface learning alone has limitations: it does not help you apply knowledge to unfamiliar scenarios, nor does it embed knowledge in long-term memory. If you rely exclusively on rote memorisation, you risk "cramming and forgetting," which can make you feel unprepared and overwhelmed.

Deep learning

Deep learning involves making connections, understanding principles, and applying them in different contexts. For example, rather than simply memorising limitation periods, deep learning means understanding *why* different areas of law have different limitation rules, how those rules interact with equitable doctrines like laches, and how limitation operates in practice when drafting pleadings or advising clients.

Deep learning makes recall easier because you are retrieving information from a network of related knowledge rather than trying to summon isolated facts. It also equips you to tackle the applied problem-solving nature of SQE questions, where you are asked not just "what is the law?" but "how does the law apply to this client's problem?"

Why this distinction matters for the SQE

The SQE is designed to test your ability to apply legal knowledge in practice, not just recite black-letter law. That means:

- You do need some surface-level memorisation (dates, figures, definitions, procedural steps).
- But you cannot pass relying on surface knowledge alone. You need deep learning to interpret client scenarios, spot issues, and choose the best legal answer.

Therefore, your preparation should balance building a factual foundation with developing conceptual understanding and application skills.

Given the nature of the SQE assessments, with the substantial amount of material that must be absorbed and retained over a lengthy period, it is likely that deep learning will yield better results. However, deep learning is not something that people naturally do; rather, it is an approach that needs to be cultivated and practised.

Tips to cultivate deep learning practices

Learn actively

You may have heard this referred to as "active learning," which simply refers to doing something with any new material you are learning, rather than simply absorbing it. For example, read mindfully – rather than just reading through the material, think about it as you read and ask yourself questions, or take small pauses to see if you can take the material and apply it to other scenarios. For example, if you are given an example, try to think of another one where the outcome would be the same, and one where the outcome would be different. You can also use this exercise to link new material with your previous learning.

EXAMPLE: Active learning from a textbook

You are learning about witness evidence and the procedure for serving witness statements. You might ask yourself what would happen if you cannot comply with the procedure. If you do not know, you can look it up, but prior to that, it is worth thinking about whether you can work it out using your existing knowledge. You have previously studied interim applications (any application to the court which happens before the final trial). These included both an application for extension of time and an application for relief from sanctions. You also remember that in some circumstances, the claimant and defendant can agree to extend the time for certain procedures without needing to ask the court. When you then learn the actions open to you if you cannot comply with the procedure for serving witness statements, you can see how these fit with your previous knowledge and the civil litigation process.

By actively engaging with what you are reading, you have revised your existing knowledge and situated your new learning within the context of the civil litigation process, making it easier for you to remember and to use both the new and the old material.

Participate: Part of active learning

If you take classes, watch lectures, or read study guides as part of your preparation for the SQE, if you are asked questions, do try to answer them. This should go without saying, but it is very easy to be lulled into thinking you know the material and can apply it *until you actually try*. Waiting to be given or just reading the answer does not yield the same learning benefits as trying the exercise. It is not unusual for students to think they have the knowledge they need and are in good shape for the assessment, only to find out on the day that they've been fooling themselves. There is an added benefit to having a go – if you get it wrong, you are much more likely to remember the correct answer than if you had not participated.

Understand the context

Placing new knowledge within the bigger picture and understanding how it fits with basic principles can really help to solidify your understanding and help you remember significant amounts of material. Particularly with law, asking why something is the way it is can both give you a deeper understanding of the rules and help you to remember them.

EXAMPLE: Contextualising knowledge – look for the why and the what

You are learning about property law and the Land Registry. Understanding what the Land Registry is for (the principles behind its formation) will help you remember the procedures and rules. This is because you can link why the procedures and rules are what they are with the key principles of what the Land Registry is meant to do.

Look for links

We've already touched on this earlier, but it is very effective for recall. Our brains work by association and can grow new connections to support whatever we are thinking about and/or practising. You might have heard this called "neuroplasticity." Looking for links between prior knowledge and new knowledge helps cement the new knowledge in your memory and refreshes the prior knowledge as well. See "Active learning from a textbook" for an example of linking previous and new knowledge.

Organise information in a way meaningful to you

This is similar to looking for links, but whilst some links will be obvious to everyone, it may be that you have experiences or thought processes specific to you that will help you to remember and recall information and how to apply it. For example, you may have had experience with a legal issue in real life that you can use to help you remember the specifics of the law and its application.

How you organise the information will affect your ability to recall it, so it is critical that the organisation method works for you. For example, some of our students like to think about how civil litigation costs work as part of the initial setting up of a claim, but some find it suits them better when thinking about settlement, and some make links with both parts of the civil litigation process.

Practise applying the knowledge with different scenarios

This has two benefits: first, the practice means you are actively learning, which helps improve both understanding and recall. Second, by applying the knowledge in different scenarios, you are fixing the principles firmly in place and then using them to explore how they can be applied. Bonus points for doing some practice that is as close to exam conditions as possible. The more you can replicate what you will need to do in an assessment, the more comfortable you will be with the actual assessment and the more you will be able to put your brain power into answering the assessment questions well, rather than getting used to a new assessment method.

TAKE A MOMENT ...

Think about your experiences of learning and assessments. When did you employ surface learning? When did you use deep learning? Have you used any of the techniques set out above before? Are there any that you would like to try?

Practical tips for absorbing and remembering material (a non-exhaustive list)

We cannot stress enough the importance of finding tips that work for you. Everyone is different; everyone has preferred learning strategies. In this section, we cover some of the most common techniques that we know work for the majority of our students, but if you have something that works for you that isn't included, that is fine! Don't stop using things you know work for you, but be aware that the sheer volume of information you need to know for the SQE and the length of time for which you need to retain it means it is probably different from assessments you may have undertaken before. The nature of the SQE assessment means that nearly all of our students need to adapt or change their previous learning and revision techniques. This is why we've also taken the unusual step of discussing some common techniques that we do *not* recommend, as, for most people, they are not effective for the volume and breadth of information that the SQE requires.

Things that make information easier to remember

We're human, and information that contains or can be linked to human interest is likely to be easier to remember. We've all had the experience where the latest shocking gossip or plot development of a favourite TV show is easier to remember than work or educational information. The deep learning techniques mentioned above are useful, but linking the relevant information with emotions, stories, or your real-life experiences will help you to remember it. Whenever you can, link the knowledge with what you know about and/or care about and find interesting. For example, the extensively reported "Wagatha Christie" trial had some sensational facts about what may have happened to some evidence on a mobile phone, making the process and duties under the disclosure stage of civil litigation proceedings much easier to remember.

TAKE A MOMENT ...

What in your real life would help you understand or remember new information of the type needed for the SQE? (TV shows, lived experience (yours or other people's), interests, stories, and the news are all potential memory aids).

Word techniques

Condensed notes

This is not the writing and re-writing of study materials warned against below, but rather the technique of extracting key information and using it as a framework for remembering the additional information required. For example, you could extract the key principles and tests for each type of interim application and record them in a document so you can see the similarities and differences to help you remember. Once you are clear on the principles and tests, you can use these to help you remember what documents are necessary.

Music

Setting verbal information to a tune and/or making information into song lyrics to be sung can aid memory and recall. The rhythm and melody of a song can make it easier to remember the order and sequencing of the information, and the phrase structure of a song can be used to put related information together (chunking – see below). For example, you could construct a song in which each verse deals with a different aspect of a topic, and the chorus is a reminder of the key principles.

Rhymes, names, stories

Making information rhyme, associating it with somebody by name, or putting it together into a story can enhance information recall. For example, imagining that you are planning to steal something, and thinking about how you could argue against the test needed to convict you, would help you to remember what the test is and how it is applied.

Chunking (categorisation)

Putting related information together into "chunks" makes it easier to remember. This can be a particularly effective technique as it reduces memory load. For example, the formalities for the court documents where you state your claim or defence (also known as "statements of case") are very similar. This means that rather than remembering all the formalities for each document separately, you can remember the formalities that apply to all the documents as one set of common requirements, then add in where each document differs as additional information.

Interleaving

Mixing up topics in your study sessions, rather than focusing on a single topic for hours, can feel more challenging, but it improves your learning by forcing your brain to discriminate between similar concepts.

Visual techniques

Mind maps (sometimes called tree and branches)

Beginning with a central concept (usually within a shape), you then draw lines out from that central concept, mapping related ideas and information. This is sometimes conceptualised as the central concept being the trunk of a tree and the related concepts branching out as, well, branches.

So you might start with "Shareholders' rights" as a central concept, then have what those rights are as the first branches, followed by the relevant principles as second branches, and finally the actions shareholders can take to enforce those rights as third branches.

Mind maps are very useful for showing the connections between information and are especially useful for chunking (see earlier for chunking).

Flowcharts

Many legal concepts and processes can be represented by flowcharts. Flowcharts are excellent for showing the order in which steps need to be taken and can enable a clear understanding of the big picture.

You can also use a flowchart to break a process down into key steps, then add related information to each step, giving both a big-picture view and a detailed view of each process stage. For example, you could think of the steps needed to transfer a property, then add the details of what happens in each step (documents, money transferred, when the transfer becomes binding, what the different types of property ownership mean).

Images and infographics

Some people find that associating information with a picture (or pictures) or representing it as an infographic helps them to remember it.

For example, showing routes of appeal and which courts are bound by precedent can be represented as a diagram with up arrows for which court appeals go to and down arrows for which court binds another court with its rulings.

Memory palace

This is a visualisation technique. You imagine a palace with numerous rooms, and you allocate the information you are trying to remember to different rooms. When you want to retrieve the information, you navigate your way around your palace to the room where it is stored. You can also use this technique to link related information; for instance, you could put everything to do with tort law in the east wing of your palace, where all the rooms are green.

You don't have to visualise a palace; you can visualise anything that helps with your recall, such as a bag with many sections or a set of bookshelves.

Techniques with time

Pomodoro

This is a time management technique to improve concentration and efficiency. You work in short, concentrated bursts, usually 25 minutes of work followed by a five-minute break. This can be an effective way to maintain concentration over long periods and to prevent procrastination and burnout.

Spaced repetition (consolidation)

This is an incredibly effective way to promote retention and recall. Given the significant amount of information the SQE requires you to recall and the length of time over which you need to retain it, it is not possible to deal with one topic and then dispense with it. Accordingly, you need to keep all your Functioning Legal Knowledge retained and available for recall. Spaced repetition strategically schedules reviews of information to optimise retention.

Some methods of spaced repetition suggest specific time periods for attempting to recall and then review the information, but you can adjust the time periods depending on your ability to recall the information (see also "Flashcards"). An initial spaced repetition plan might be to review the information two to three days after initially learning it, then at a week, then at ten days to two weeks, gradually increasing the interval between review periods or shortening it if you are struggling to recall the information. It is important that you first attempt to recall the information without looking it up or revising it. You can then see where the gaps in your knowledge are, revise those, and test again.

Regularly revise and review (consolidation)

This is a variant on spaced repetition – some people prefer having set revise and review periods rather than increasing or decreasing the time between reviews. Whilst spaced repetition is probably more effective for most people, the key thing is that you keep all your Functioning Legal Knowledge "warm" – that is, available for recall as necessary. For nearly everyone, this will involve some kind of continual revising and reviewing process.

Techniques that work well with other people

Flashcards

These are physical or electronic cards with information on both sides – one side has a concept, question, or relevant word, and the other side has the definition of the word, explanation of the concept, or answer to the question. You can then use the cards to test yourself or, if studying with peers, each other. The act of making the cards can help you remember the information, and you could team up with peers to each make cards for one area, which you then all share and use. This is quite a time-consuming revision method, so teaming up in this way can be more effective.

Flashcards can also be used to support spaced repetition (see earlier). After you have used them to review, you can organise the cards into different boxes. For cards where you were wrong about the information, put them in a box for more frequent review (until you get the information right). For information you got correct, move those cards into a box to review less frequently. This technique is sometimes called the Leitner System of Revision, after its inventor, Sebastian Leitner.

There are several free applications you can use to help you make flashcards, but do check the output is accurate (and no hallucinations have crept in) if you are using artificial intelligence (AI).

Be the teacher

A good way to assess whether you understand something is to see if you can explain it to someone else so they can understand it. The process of explaining and answering any questions they may have will help you retain and recall the information. This is something that you can do with friends or family, or you could work with your peers, and each take an element of a topic to explain to everyone else. However, this can be particularly effective if you are explaining legal concepts and processes to people without any legal background, as they will not be able to help you explain or have background knowledge to rely on if you forget to mention something or are not clear in your explanation.

Study groups and peer support

Study groups and teaming up with one or more peers can be very powerful. First, making a study commitment to other people can be motivational, as they can hold you accountable for getting the work done. You can also find ways to split the work between you for everyone's benefit (see "Flashcards"). Even just working by yourself whilst also working as a group (either online or in real life) can be motivational. This can be especially effective if members of a group are all working individually but using the Pomodoro technique (see earlier) together, with one person acting as timekeeper. Everyone can say at the start of the session what they hope to achieve and report back at the end of the session how they got on.

Peer review and peer marking are also effective techniques for testing yourself (peers can be more objective than you may be about your work). You can support each other emotionally, motivationally, and practically by helping each other understand concepts. Peer review/marking can be especially useful for the SQE2 skills. For example, reviewing each other's drafting will help you to understand the SRA requirements, as well as giving you an idea of whether or not you are meeting them.

Testing yourself

Before, during, and after

There is some evidence that testing yourself before, during, and after learning is beneficial to long-term recall. Testing before you begin learning establishes what, if anything, you know about a topic; testing during learning helps to fix the knowledge through active learning; and testing after establishes what information you have retained and where you need to spend more time to ensure you can recall it.

There are various ways to test yourself (some of which we have already covered), and some that we cover below.

Blurting

This is where you write down everything you can remember about a topic, before revising any knowledge. You can then see what you know, fill in any gaps, and correct any misunderstandings with your revision. Blurting can be used effectively with spaced repetition (see above) as the initial stage in reviewing what you already know.

Feynman technique

This is a variation on the "be the teacher" technique, named after Professor Richard Feynman. It involves simplifying complex information by breaking it down into basic terms, as if you were explaining it to a child. You choose a topic, explain it as simply as you can, and then identify any elements you missed or struggled to explain simply. You can then check the material to improve your explanation, continuing to make it even simpler if possible.

This technique can take a significant amount of time, so it may not be practicable to use for everything.

Assessment question practice

Ultimately, testing yourself in the way you will be tested in the assessment will give you the best outcome because it allows you to refine your assessment technique. However, just practising MCQs without having deep learning and a proper understanding to draw on is unlikely to be sufficient, as explained earlier. You will learn the answers to various MCQs, but it is unlikely that these will come up in the same form in the actual assessment. So whilst MCQ practice is important, as is practising in conditions as close to the assessment conditions as possible (including timed, closed-book practice), it will be more effective if you invest time in gaining the relevant Functioning Legal Knowledge first. There are various compilations of MCQs that you can use to test yourself. The SRA has also published a number of example questions which you can access on their website.

The more accustomed you are to attempting MCQs under SQE assessment conditions, the easier you should find the actual assessments, as you will be used to the conditions and well-practised in what you need to do on the day.

This sort of question practice can also be done with peers, where you mark each other's work. It is key that you not only get the right answer, but that you also understand why it is the right answer and why the other answers are not the best for the fact pattern. It is worth taking a little extra time and ensuring that you have the requisite understanding.

Interleaving

This is the practice of mixing up topics and/or subject areas and/or revision strategies. If you want to make your review and revision process more challenging, you can do so by moving from one subject area to another or from one topic to an unrelated one. This is also good practice for SQE1 as each of the two papers covers a different combination of subjects, and the questions on each subject are mixed up within each paper, not contained in discrete sections. For example, there is no business law and practice section followed by a contract law section – MCQs on all topics covered in each paper are mixed up.

Other ideas

This technique is more unusual, but you may want to try it.

Anchoring

This is the technique of associating knowledge/information with something that you can recreate to help you recall it. This could include smells (for example, using an essential oil or specific perfume while you are learning, which you then smell again to help you recall the information), places (for example, you always learn in the same place and then, when needing to recall information, imagine yourself in that place), or whatever anchoring point works for you. If you plan to use this technique, make sure you check that you will be able to have access to your anchor, whatever it is, while you are sitting the assessment. Please see the section on "What to expect on the day" to assess whether you would be allowed to take your anchor or access it in the assessment centre.

TAKE A MOMENT ...

Is there anything we have not included here that helps you understand and remember information?

Important note: we have included the most common techniques and those with evidence that they are effective. There are other techniques, and if these work for you, please do continue to use them. What techniques work for you will depend on how you prefer to learn, but also on how long each technique takes you. Given the amount of information you need to learn and recall for the SQE, it may not be possible to use time-consuming techniques for all of your learning. You will need to be very careful that the time you are spending is proportionate to how much you are learning and how much you need to learn and recall overall.

Common techniques we DO NOT recommend for the SQE

Re-writing or continually re-reading study materials or highlighting notes or study materials without actively using the knowledge is unlikely to prepare you adequately for the SQE. Unless you have a photographic memory (can remember and recall information after reading it once), just re-writing and reading study materials are unlikely to create deep learning, and the same goes for highlighting without taking further action. This is partly because the volume of information you need to retain means that it is not time-efficient to repeatedly re-write and re-read, and partly because these techniques are unlikely to result in deep learning. There is simply too much information for most people to be able to cram and learn at the last minute, so relying on surface learning is not advised.

Your learning and revision should be challenging. If you find your learning, memorisation, and recall easy, change the techniques and/or move to a different knowledge area that you find more difficult. You may feel that you are making progress because you have pages of written and/or highlighted notes, but you can only get an accurate feel for how well prepared you are by attempting SQE exam-style questions. However, repeatedly attempting MCQs (without undertaking other learning) is not an effective way to learn for the SQE. Just practising MCQs encourages surface learning rather than a deeper understanding of the information. You need this deeper understanding to enable you to apply the knowledge to different scenarios, which is what you need to be able to do for the SQE.

Key takeaways

You need to learn and be able to recall significant amounts of information for the SQE.

Find and use learning, revision, and recall techniques that work for you.

Active learning (doing something with the information) will help you remember better than passive learning (reading and re-reading or taking notes from learning materials).

You have limited time to learn a lot of information. Make sure whatever techniques you are using take an appropriate amount of time for the amount you learn.

Common pitfalls to avoid

Cramming without consolidation: knowledge fades quickly if not revisited.

Focusing only on familiar topics: it's tempting to revise what you already know, but the SQE will test you across the syllabus.

Overloading on detail: you do not need every case name or statutory subsection; focus on principles and application.

Neglecting exam technique: knowing the law is not enough; you must practise applying it in timed, multiple-choice conditions.

Identifying your learning preferences to aid your approach to SQE1

Identifying how you like to learn

Preparing for the SQE can feel overwhelming: the breadth of material, the pressure of time, and the need to recall and apply information quickly are all significant challenges. One way to make your revision more efficient and sustainable is to understand how you like to learn best. Knowing your preferences does not mean you are locked into a single method of study, and it is important to note that you can learn equally well however the information is provided to you. Further, most education experts recommend learning with a variety of styles to improve recall. However, aligning your revision techniques with your learning preferences may help you to feel confident and avoid burnout.

Visual, auditory, and kinaesthetic learners

Although most people learn through a mix of approaches, researchers often describe three broad categories of learning styles:

Visual learners

Visual learners prefer images, diagrams, colour coding, and spatial organisation. They may find dense blocks of text difficult to process, but will thrive when information is organised into flowcharts, mind maps, or timelines. For SQE preparation, visual learners often benefit from making diagrams of legal processes (e.g., steps in civil procedure) or colour coding different areas of law in their notes.

Auditory learners

Auditory learners prefer hearing the information. They may find lectures, podcasts, group discussions, or even "teaching" the material to someone else particularly effective. For the SQE, this could mean recording yourself explaining key principles and playing it back, or joining a study group where you can talk through practice questions out loud.

Kinaesthetic learners

Kinaesthetic learners prefer to learn by *doing*. They like hands-on practice, movement, and active engagement with material rather than passive reading or listening. In the SQE context, kinaesthetic learners might focus on repeatedly answering practice MCQs under timed conditions, role-playing client scenarios, or even physically moving flashcards around a desk to create sequences and connections.

Self-assessment techniques

How do you know which learning style fits you best? Whilst there are formal questionnaires (for example; VARK), you can also learn a lot through self-reflection:

- Think about past study experiences: when have you felt most engaged?
- Notice what frustrates you most – do you find it hard to sit still and read notes? Do you switch off during long audio recordings?

- Experiment: take one topic (e.g., contract remedies) and study it three different ways – a diagram, a podcast-style explanation, and practice questions. Which one feels most natural and helps you recall the information more easily later?

Remember, you don't have to fit neatly into one category. Most candidates are a blend. The key is to identify your strongest tendencies so you can play to them while also stretching yourself with other methods when useful.

Adapting revision strategies

Once you have a sense of your preferred learning style, you can tailor your study techniques to make them more effective. Here are some targeted strategies for SQE revision:

For visual learners

- Create mind maps for each area of law showing how topics connect.
- Use colour-coded sticky notes or highlighters to distinguish between procedural rules, statutory provisions, and case law.
- Turn lists into diagrams (e.g., a flowchart of the conveyancing process).

For auditory learners

- Record summaries of your notes and listen to them while walking or commuting.
- Discuss tricky topics with peers in study groups.
- Read example questions aloud and explain your reasoning verbally before writing down the answer.

For kinaesthetic learners

- Do as many practice questions as possible under timed conditions.
- Act out procedural steps (e.g., serve a "mock" claim form and walk through what happens next).
- Use physical flashcards to test yourself by sorting, matching, or sequencing.

Tailoring your revision does not mean excluding other methods. Someone who prefers visual learning may still benefit from practice questions, just as someone who prefers kinaesthetic learning may find diagrams useful. The aim is to make your dominant preferred style the foundation of your approach while still mixing in other methods to ensure flexibility.

Overcoming usual challenges

Even once you've identified your preferred learning style, be aware of hurdles.

Over-reliance on one style

If you only ever use your preferred method, you may neglect important exam skills. For example, visual learners still need to practise timed question-answering, not just draw diagrams.

Time constraints

Some styles take longer to prepare. For instance, creating elaborate diagrams or recording audio notes can be time-consuming. Use these strategically and balance them with faster revision techniques.

Exam format mismatch

The SQE assessments are text-based and time pressured. This means that even if you prefer auditory or kinaesthetic learning, you must adapt your methods to prepare for answering written multiple-choice questions on screen efficiently.

Stress and fatigue

Under exam conditions, your preferred style may not be available. A kinaesthetic learner, for example, cannot physically "move" during the exam. Practising other styles ensures you remain adaptable.

Final thoughts

Understanding your preferred learning style is not about putting yourself in a box; it's about giving yourself the self-awareness to make smarter revision choices. By identifying whether you prefer visual, auditory, or kinaesthetic learning, you can focus your study energy where it will have the most impact while still developing flexibility for the exam environment.

The SQE is not just a test of legal knowledge – it is also a test of stamina, discipline, and strategic preparation. Aligning your revision with your natural preferences is one way to make the process more manageable and effective, helping you to retain information and walk into the exam room with greater confidence.

3

SQE2

The SQE2 assessments

The SQE2 assessments are designed to test your legal skills and application of fundamental legal rules and principles. You are expected to demonstrate the competency of a competent newly qualified solicitor on the first day as a solicitor (a "day one solicitor"). A common misconception is that SQE2 only assesses legal skills: in fact, half of the marks are awarded for your performance of the relevant skill and half for your application of the relevant Functioning Legal Knowledge. This is the reason why many candidates choose to sit SQE2 at the first opportunity after passing SQE1, while their FLK is still fresh in their minds.

The 16 mini-assessments (or "stations" as the SRA refers to them) that make up SQE2 are taken over five half days: three half days are dedicated to written skills and two to oral skills. The SQE2 assessments are closed-book assessments, in the same way as for SQE1.

The SQE2 assessments are usually very different from anything candidates have done before – for example, for some of them, you need to be able to handwrite for up to 25 minutes. If you need reasonable adjustments, you should apply for these when you first register for the SQE (see "Requesting reasonable adjustments for SQE assessments" in Part 2, pages 44–45).

Written skills

The written skills are legal drafting, legal writing, legal research, and case and matter analysis. On each written skills assessment half day, you will have a short assessment in each of the four written skills. On day one, you will undertake assessments in the context of Dispute Resolution or Criminal Law and Practice (Criminal Litigation). On

DOI: 10.4324/9781003639671-4

day two, it will be Property Practice (including money laundering) or Wills and the Administration of Estates (Wills and Intestacy, Probate Administration and Practice); on day three, you will undertake all assessments in the context of Business Law and Practice, including organisations, rules and procedures (including money laundering and financial services). This means you need to be prepared to sit any of the written assessments in any of the five FLK areas.

The SQE2 written assessments are undertaken in Pearson Vue test centres (in a similar way to SQE1). See "Booking the SQE1 assessments" in Part 2, pages 41–47.

Oral skills

The oral skills are interview and attendance note/legal analysis, and advocacy. On each oral skills assessment half day, you will have one advocacy and one interview assessment, each in a different legal context. The four FLK areas assessed in the oral skills are Dispute Resolution, Property Practice (including money laundering), Criminal Law and Practice (Criminal Litigation), and Wills and the Administration of Estates (Wills and Intestacy, Probate Administration and Practice).

The oral assessments take place in person in a small number of cities in England and Wales (at the time of writing, London, Cardiff, Birmingham, and Manchester). This means that many candidates must travel to sit SQE2 and, unlike SQE1, it is not possible to sit the oral assessments overseas.

In addition to the six separately assessed written and oral skills, you will be assessed in the skill of negotiation at least once in each sit of SQE2. Negotiation may arise in the interview and attendance note/legal analysis and/or in case and matter analysis and/or in legal writing. It will not be obvious that you need to address negotiation, so you need to be aware of the skills in which it may appear and address it appropriately.

Ethics and Professional Conduct are pervasive throughout SQE2 and will not be signposted, so you will need to spot any professional and/or ethical issues and address them appropriately when they arise.

You are expected to demonstrate the competency of a competent newly qualified solicitor on the first day as a solicitor (a "day one solicitor") in the SQE2 assessments. However, you are not expected to know or address details that a day one solicitor would need to look up. As such, for all skills except legal research, you will be provided, as part of your assessment materials, with materials that a day one solicitor would look up. You may not take any other books or notes into the SQE2 assessments.

There is a single pass mark for SQE2 (as a whole): your marks for each of the 16 stations are aggregated to give your final mark. You do not receive a mark for each of the individual parts of your assessment.

You can access helpful performance indicators (guidance on what the SRA considers competent for each skill) and sample questions for SQE2 on the SRA's SQE website.

Examinable law in SQE2

A key aspect of the assessment specification for SQE2 is a statement of the FLK that is examinable in SQE2. This is set out in Annex 1 to the SQE2 Assessment Specification. In many ways, the examinable law is very similar to that in SQE1; however, there are some key aspects that are not examinable in SQE2. For example, key aspects of Constitutional and Administrative Law you will have studied for SQE1 will not arise in SQE2.

As in SQE1, the cut-off for examinable law is four months before the start of the relevant assessment window. The precise date of this cut-off is included with the assessment dates on the SRA's SQE website.

The SQE2 written assessments

We start with information relevant to all the SQE2 written assessments, along with general advice and tips to help you tackle them. We then give an overview of each assessment, along with specific tips for approaching that specific assessment.

How you take them

The written assessments are computer-based using the Pearson Vue assessment platform. This is a purpose-built computer-based assessment platform, and it does not have the functionality you are probably used to from your word-processing programmes. It is very important that you familiarise yourself with the platform and how to use it, including the spell check tool, copy and paste and highlighting functionality. You can read more about the platform and how to use it on the SRA's SQE website, and the SRA has made it available for you to try with its SQE2 written skills assessment example questions.

The exam environment

The exam environment is tightly controlled, and you are not allowed to bring anything in unless it is classed as a comfort item, such as a crutch. You can see a list of comfort items on the SRA's SQE website and you should notify the SRA if you require such items as part of the reasonable adjustments procedure. You get an online calculator, a pen, and a small dry wipe whiteboard on which to make notes. The exams are closed book, although you will be provided with anything a day one solicitor would need to look up.

For what to expect on the SQE2 days, please see "The practicalities: Before, during, and after the exam" on pages 47–51 in Part 2 and the SRA's SQE website. You can also watch a Pearson Vue video about SQE2 on the Pearson Vue website (http://pearsonvue.com).

Ways to prepare for the SQE2 written assessments

These are suggestions that are applicable to all written assessments.

Buddy up and/or form a study group

Having someone else who understands the SQE2 marking criteria and the relevant assessment to act as a critical friend is very powerful. If you can find a study buddy and mark each other's practice questions, that will help you get another view on your work and also understand how the marking criteria work in practice.

Try some different forms of note-taking until you find one that works for you

You will have a small whiteboard on which you can take notes in the assessments, and you can also write notes in the answer space in the test environment. If you decide to put notes in the answer space, remember to check you have removed everything by proofreading at the end. However, making notes this way can be very helpful, as it creates a structure for your work that you can then use to write up your document.

There are several different ways of note-taking, and you need to find those that work for you. It might be that different methods work for you for different assessments. Some ideas to try include:

1. Using headings and accumulating relevant notes underneath. For example, you could use the client's objectives as headings and then put relevant information and law under the relevant heading.
2. Creating a table – this can be particularly helpful for situations where there are different options, so you can compare them to see how each would meet the client's objectives, offer the client choice, and identify where you need more information. For example, you could write out a table with the first column containing the different limbs of a legal test, then put the relevant information next to each limb to help establish what advice you should give. An alternative example might be to set out different negotiation strategies in the first column and then populate the other columns with relevant facts and client objectives for each strategy to help you plan tactics.
3. You can also create a standard structure with headings and then make notes in the relevant places. This can work well for drafting, where you structure the document, make notes, and use those notes to complete the drafting within the standard document structure. For example, you could set out the expected contents of a particulars of claim in headings, then make relevant notes before populating the draft particulars of claim and proofreading the final version.
4. Highlighting in documents – this can save time over typing notes but runs the risk that you will forget relevant facts or spend too much time flicking backwards and forwards through the documents to find the information you have highlighted.

TAKE A MOMENT ...

Which ways of making notes will you try or do you use now? Which will you use for each of the written SQE2 assessments?

Timed practice

These are highly time-pressured exams, so practising in timed conditions is very important so you are used to managing your time before the actual assessment. Suggestions for time allocation are included below for each assessment.

Make sure you plan

We cannot overemphasise the importance of planning, both for deciding on a sensible structure and also for making sure you haven't left out anything vital. When you first start practising, you may want to spend longer on planning, speeding up as you get more used to the types of assessment.

Speed up your reading

You may find that it is taking you a significant amount of time to read the instructions and documents and extract the necessary information. Being able to do this quickly is a skill that you need for the SQE assessments, and you can improve by practising. If you are having trouble with this, it is well worth putting aside some time for practice.

Try a timed attempt in the SRA Pearson Vue assessment platform

Please see earlier for information about this. Use the SRA's exemplar answer to compare to your attempt, but also to examine how the exemplar meets the marking criteria.

Ensure your FLK is current, right for the context of the assessment day, and revise it as necessary

Fifty percent of the marks for the skills assessments are for the skill, and 50% of them are for applying your FLK correctly and comprehensively to the assessment scenario. As described earlier, the FLK needed for SQE2 is a subset of that learnt for SQE1. This means you need to keep the FLK needed for SQE2 "warm" and revise it as necessary. Please see "Tips for absorbing and recalling significant amounts of information" in Part 2, pages 57–771 for ideas on how to do this. It is important to check in advance which legal contexts will form the backdrop to the assessment on any given day so that you have the relevant area of law fresh in your mind. Remember that half of the marks for the assessment will be awarded for your understanding of the relevant law, so the marker will be looking for the quality of your understanding of the legal points as much as they will be analysing the way in which you exercise the legal skills.

Remember to watch for professional conduct, ethical issues, and negotiation

Unflagged (you will be expected to recognise them without being told) professional conduct and ethical issues may be tested in any of the SQE2 assessments.

Negotiation will be tested at least once (and may come up more than once) in any of the interview and attendance note, case and matter analyses, and/or legal writing assessments.

Prepare for the logistics

Sleep, food, and hydration are important. If you need to travel, make sure you have somewhere where you can get a good rest the night before and that you have everything you need to put yourself in the best mental and physical state to take the assessments.

There are extensive identity checks to undertake for the SQE2 assessments, so make sure you are early to give yourself time to undertake any ID checks, so you are not causing yourself unnecessary stress. Please see "The practicalities: Before, during, and after the exam" in Part 2 (pages 47–50) for more details and note that you may need to inform the SRA SQE Candidate Services Team by particular deadlines if certain circumstances apply to you (e.g., carrying religious items, reasonable adjustments for comfort items or physical adjustments, etc.).

Keep calm

Going into the assessment calm and well prepared will give you the best possible chance of doing well. Once in the assessment, do not be tempted to miss out on any of the important stages we recommend (for example, planning).

Do not correct small errors at the expense of completing the assessment

You should aim for your writing to be fault-free, but do balance this with the need to submit a complete piece of work in the available timeframe: do not take time to correct non-material errors at the expense of finishing the assessment.

Check your work

If you can, leave time to check your work. You should aim to allow a small amount of time at the end of the assessment to proofread what you have written.

SRA marking criteria common to the written assessments

Fifty percent of the marks are for the skill, and 50% for your FLK (see "Examinable law in SQE2"). This is why it is so important to keep your FLK remembered and in mind.

Where marking criteria are specific to an assessment, they are considered under the appropriate assessment heading. Where the criteria are relevant to all the written assessments, they are considered here. For the avoidance of doubt, all relevant criteria are listed under the relevant assessment headings, but discussion of the common criteria is provided here to prevent repetition.

Skills criteria

1. Use clear, concise, and acceptable language.

   The SRA says this includes using clear, succinct, and accurate language; avoiding unnecessary technical terms where they are not appropriate for the recipient; and using an acceptable style of communication for the situation and recipient.
2. Identify relevant facts.

   This is a key skill for all of the SQE2 assessments. To be able to give accurate legal advice, you need to understand what is relevant, both regarding the law and what is important to the client. For example, if a client would like to leave his estate to his stepchildren in his will, it will be important to take note of whether the client has adopted the stepchildren in order to determine how the will should be drafted.
3. Provide client-focused advice.

   You always need to tailor your advice to the recipient, which means viewing the issue from the perspective of what the client wants to achieve, not just from a legal perspective. For example, it may not be possible to achieve the client's objectives by relying on the law alone; negotiation or mediation may be more successful in achieving the client's objectives.

Application of law

The assessment criteria for application of law refer to:

1. legally correct,
2. legally comprehensive; and
3. ethics and professional conduct.
1. The SRA has released further non-exhaustive guidance on what application of law looks like to be legally correct and comprehensive.
    - Identifying relevant legal principles.
    - Applying legal principles to factual issues to produce a solution which best addresses a client's needs and reflects the client's commercial or personal circumstances, including as part of a negotiation.
    - Interpreting, evaluating, and applying the results of research.
    - Ensuring that advice is informed by appropriate legal analysis and identifies the consequences of different options.
    - Drafting documents that are legally effective.
    - Applying understanding, critical thinking, and analysis to solve problems.
    - Assessing information to identify key issues and risks.
    - Recognising inconsistencies and gaps in information.
    - Evaluating the quality and reliability of information.
    - Using multiple sources of information to make effective judgements.
    - Reaching reasoned decisions supported by relevant information.
    - Identifying any ethical and professional conduct issues and exercising judgement to resolve them honestly and with integrity.

A brief note on the difference between correct and comprehensive application of the law

The SRA has stated that how "correct" and "comprehensive" is interpreted depends on the academic judgement of the examiner of each assessment, whose interpretation will be informed by the Statement of Solicitor Competence and the FLK for SQE2. The guidance states that identifying and applying legal principles correctly to the specific facts is likely to be awarded under legally correct, while the extent to which a candidate has done this and provided a comprehensive analysis of the legal principles would be awarded under legally comprehensive. If the legal principles are made explicit in the question, correct application of the legal principles to the facts may be awared under legally correct. Giving a comprehensive analysis of the principles and of any other legal issues that arise on the facts may be awarded under legally comprehensive.

If a question involves any ethics and professional conduct issues, candidates must identify the issue(s) and exercise judgement to resolve them honestly and with integrity.

Presentation, spelling, and grammar

The Pearson Vue assessment platform, in which you will take the SQE2 written assessments, has much more limited functionality than Word or LibreOffice (or other word-processing programmes). For example, at the time of writing, the SRA was only beginning to trial a spell check function in SQE2 written assessments. As such, at the time of writing, the SRA states that candidates should not lose marks for spelling mistakes that:

- do not impact on the legal accuracy, clarity, and/or certainty of the written text; and
- would normally be flagged by spell-check functionality, noting that spell check would not, for example, necessarily flag errors in names, addresses, dates, or values.

Similarly, candidates should not lose marks for grammatical errors that:

- do not impact on the legal accuracy, clarity, and/or certainty of the written text, noting that, for example, grammatical errors in the use of tense could have such an impact; and
- do not make the written text inaccessible to the intended reader.

Nor should candidates lose marks for poor formatting, given the lack of formatting support on the test platform and the time restraints under which they are working. However, with the trial of a spell check tool, this guidance may change, so it is important that you check the most up to date guidance on the SRA's SQE website.

TAKE A MOMENT ...

Make a list of all the common errors that would make a difference to the legal effect of a document. For example, names, amounts, dates, how to sign, and so on. Prioritise these points when checking your work in the assessment.

Legal drafting

Before reading this part, please make sure you have read the general information about SQE2 at the start of this chapter. This covers SQE2 information that will not be repeated here.

Difference between legal writing and legal drafting

Legal writing is clear communication about legal matters, for example, a letter of advice. Legal drafting is writing that creates or fulfils legal obligations and/or requirements, for example, a contract for sale or statements of case for litigation.

The drafting assessments

You will have three 45-minute drafting assessments, one each day of the written skills examinations.

During the drafting assessment, you will need to read carefully through a set of instructions and probably some additional documents. The instructions could be from a law firm colleague (like a supervising partner), a client, or simply set out as instructions for the assessment.

You may be asked to amend a precedent (a standard document template), a document drafted by someone else, or to free draft – drafting from scratch. You could be asked to draft all or some of a document, and you may be asked to combine amending something already drafted with free drafting. For example, you could be asked to amend a contract, partly by amending some clauses that have already been drafted and partly by drafting some new clauses from scratch.

It is a very time-pressured assessment, so you need to find timings that work for you and be disciplined with your use of time. As a rough guide to timing, you could take five minutes for reading, five minutes for planning, 30 minutes for drafting, and five minutes for checking and proofreading. But you may find you prefer to take slightly longer planning (and you can even plan in the answer space), which cuts down on the time you need to spend drafting. If you do choose to plan or make notes in the answer space, you need to ensure you proofread and take out anything you do not want to be included in the finished version.

The SRA marking criteria and requirements (these are all taken from the SRA's SQE website)

Assessment objective: You must demonstrate that you are able to draft a legal document or parts of a legal document for a client.

Skills

1. Use clear, precise, concise and acceptable language.
2. Structure the document appropriately and logically.

How the document is structured will depend on what it is and what it is trying to achieve. Some documents have a set structure dictated by legal rules. It is important to take time to plan a logical structure that makes the document easy to follow. For example, in a commercial contract, any significant amount of technical information should be contained in schedules, not in the operative part of the contract.

Application of law

1. Draft a document which is legally correct.
2. Draft a document which is legally comprehensive.
3. Identify any ethical and professional conduct issues and exercise judgement to resolve them honestly and with integrity.

Negotiation will not be examined in the drafting assessments.

The types of documents you may be asked to draft

The SRA has not released a list of documents. Therefore, you may be asked to draft any relevant document. This is why it is important to understand and use the principles of good drafting rather than to try and memorise lots of different documents. However, it is sensible to be aware of the usual structure and potential contents of common documents. For example, a particulars of claim (the document setting out a claimant's case in a civil litigation matter) should follow a prescribed format, contain only facts, and cover the key legal elements of duty, breach, causation, and loss. Similarly, a commercial contract needs to cover background, defined terms, date, who is contracting, what obligations and rights the parties have, whether there are any warranties or indemnities, relevant standard clauses (like governing law and jurisdiction), how the contract could be terminated, schedules and appropriate execution clauses. For example, some documents need to be signed as a deed which means that additional formalities apply.

What makes a good piece of drafting?

Your drafting should be clear, concise, well-structured and easy to read for its intended audience. It should have the correct legal effect and consider any client concerns (even if the client has not realised that they may be concerns). It should avoid legal jargon unless it is necessary or accepted modern practice (for example, it is common to include a section called "Recitals" in a commercial contract).

Hints and tips for drafting

Keep your FLK warm

Remember 50% of the marks are on your FLK – keep it warm from SQE1 and revise any areas you feel necessary.

Everyone drafts differently

Everyone has a drafting style, and two different pieces of drafting can both be equally valid. If you are meeting the SRA marking criteria, you should get the marks. There is not one and only one correct way to draft a document, unless it is set out in legal rules such as the Civil Procedure Rules.

Focus on the SRA marking criteria

You may be familiar with ways of drafting from your studies or from legal work you have undertaken. For the purposes of SQE2, you should stick as closely as possible to the SRA marking criteria, even if that means departing from what your employer or teacher recommends.

Practise in exam conditions

Make sure you know how to use the Pearson Vue platform and have practised with it until you are confident and comfortable.

Read instructions

Read any instructions carefully and make sure you incorporate them into the document.

Tailor your drafting

Tailor your drafting to the recipient – a sophisticated corporate client might be expected to be more familiar with legal jargon (even so, please keep jargon to a minimum).

Watch boiler plate!

Beware boiler plate (standard clauses like governing law or jurisdiction clauses). Make sure they are necessary and do what the client requires.

Know structures and legal requirements

Know the structure and legal requirements for common documents in each area. For example, statements of case in Dispute Resolution, wills in Wills and the Administration of Estates (Wills and Intestacy, Probate Administration and Practice), applications in Criminal Law and Practice (Criminal Litigation), contracts of sale in Property Practice (including money laundering) and contracts and board minutes in Business Law and Practice, including organisations, rules and procedures (including money laundering and financial services).

Potentially memorise small, key texts

If you can, you may also want to memorise small, key texts, for example, the wording for a statement of truth. Unless you have an amazing memory, you are unlikely to be able to remember large chunks of text, but do not worry, thinking logically and practising the principles of good drafting should be sufficient.

TAKE A MOMENT ...

Make a list of common documents and their structures, along with any small, prescribed text that you would like to remember. If you have not begun preparing for the SQE2 yet, save this exercise for later.

Case and matter analysis

Before reading this part, please make sure you have read the general SQE2 information at the start of this chapter. This covers SQE2 information that will not be repeated here.

The case and matter analysis assessment

There are three 60-minute case and matter analysis assessments, one on each day of the written assessments. You will need to read through the instructions and additional case study documents carefully. You will then need to produce a written report for a partner providing a legal analysis of the case, together with client-focused advice.

Sixty minutes is not long, and you may like to try: five minutes to read and identify (note them down) the key issues and the client's objectives; five minutes to think about and note down the relevant law and rules for the identified issues; five to ten minutes to read the documents and pick out the key relevant facts/issues; five to ten minutes to write out a plan for your report (the planning stage is vital). You then have 20 to 30 minutes to write your report and five minutes to proofread it and check for tone, legal jargon, and so on. Whilst you may find these timings work for you, they may not, and it will also depend on the assessment questions. You will need to work out timings that work for you (see tips, below).

The SRA marking criteria and requirements (these are all taken from the SRA's SQE website)

Assessment objective: You need to demonstrate that you are able to produce a written report to a partner giving a legal analysis of the case and client-focused advice.

Skills

1. Identify relevant facts.
2. Provide client-focused advice (i.e advice which demonstrates an understanding of the problem from the client's point of view and what the client wants to achieve, not just from a legal perspective).
3. Use clear, precise, concise and acceptable language.

Application of law

1. Apply the law correctly to the client's situation.
2. Apply the law comprehensively to the client's situation.
3. Identify any ethical and professional conduct issues and exercise judgement to resolve them honestly and with integrity.

The Case and Matter Analysis assessment may also test your knowledge of negotiation. For example, client-focused advice may include considering negotiation, or setting out potential negotiation outcomes and tactics/strategies.

What makes a good case and matter analysis

Consider this from the point of view of the law firm partner for whom you are working. Your report needs to be accurate, tailored to the client, and easy to read and understand. Crucially, you need to be clear on the issue(s) and provide advice that best fits with the client's objectives. Where more than one option is available, examine the merits of each and ideally give an opinion on which fits the client's objectives best.

Hints and tips for your case and matter analysis

FLK!

Remember 50% of the marks are on your FLK – keep it warm from SQE1 and revise any areas you feel necessary.

Stick closely to the SRA marking criteria

You may be familiar with various ways of report writing from your studies or from your legal work. For the purposes of SQE2, please stick as closely as possible to the requirements of the SRA marking criteria, even if this means departing from your employer's or teacher's recommendations.

Stay flexible on the format and tone of the report

Whilst the purpose of the assessment is to provide a report for a partner, you should be prepared to be flexible, as the partner may have specific requests or want the report presented in a particular format. For example, the SRA example uses the report as the basis of a letter of advice for the client, so the writing ideally needs to be appropriate for the client. Keep an eye on what the report is going to be used for and give as much attention as possible to anything you are told about the client and their needs and wants. For example, is the client familiar with these sorts of legal issues? If not, you may need to provide a more detailed explanation with your advice.

Make sure you stay on point with your advice

Your report should address the client's concerns and not include general or extraneous information or recommendations. Ensure you are advising, not simply repeating what is in the case and matter analysis documents. Address all the questions you are asked to consider in the instructions from the partner – if you need more information, then you should say so in your answer, explaining the information you require and the reason you need it.

Remember negotiation (and ethics and professional conduct)

You may need to include strategies and options for negotiation in your report. It is also important to watch out for unflagged issues of professional conduct and ethics. You may want to have some standard negotiation strategies and options memorised for the assessments. Where you set out options for the client's consideration in your report, you should clearly set out the advantages and disadvantages of each option.

Make your report as easy to read and understand as possible

You can use subheadings and try to write in short sentences and paragraphs to aid clarity. As set out under "Use clear, precise, concise, and acceptable language," avoid jargon, including legal jargon and technical legal terms.

Sixty minutes is not long...

It is vital that you remain aware of the time, and you will need to work out your own ideal set of timings. You can try the suggested timings above, but you will need to adapt these depending on your preferences, abilities, and the questions on the day.

Make sure you practise!

The best way (in fact, the only way) to work out how long things take you is to attempt questions under timed conditions. The SRA provides one question for you to try, but you can make up some of your own. This works best if you work with other candidates and create questions for each other.

Legal research

Before reading this section, please make sure you have read the general SQE2 information at the start of this chapter. This covers SQE2 information that will not be repeated here.

The legal research assessment

There are three 60-minute legal research assessments, one on each day of the written assessments. You will be given an email from a partner which asks you to research an issue or issues so that the partner can report back to the client, and a selection of legal sources. You are not necessarily drawing on pre-existing knowledge; some of the legal information may be unfamiliar. The legal sources will be made up of a combination of primary sources (the law itself – for example, extracts from statutes or judgments) and secondary sources (commentary on the law – for example, practitioners' texts). You will need to produce a written note explaining your legal reasoning and the key sources you have relied on, as well as the advice the partner should give the client.

Again, you will need to work out the timings that work for you; timings will partly be determined by your strengths and partly by the question on the day. You could start by trying to take roughly 20 minutes to read the question and the sources and plan your answer, 30 to 35 minutes writing your answer, and five to ten minutes proofreading and checking your answer.

Important:

- You do not need to produce a research trail.
- Some of the legal sources supplied may not be relevant to the issue/issues (i.e. there could be sources designed to mislead you).
- The subject matter of the research will be within the broad area of practice in which the assessment is based, but may be outside the scope of the FLK (which is why you need to research it).

The SRA marking criteria and requirements (these are all taken from the SRA's SQE website)

Assessment objective: You must demonstrate that you are able to conduct legal research from a variety of resources provided and produce a written report.

Skills

1. Identify and use relevant sources and information.

This is the heart of the matter – you need to be able to quickly pick out the legal and factual points relevant to the issue or issues and synthesise them into accurate, appropriate, and easy-to-read advice, explaining your legal reasoning and citing the key sources on which you are relying.

2. Provide advice which is client-focused and addresses the client's problem.

Remember, this can include non-legal advice such as trying to come to an agreed solution without involving the law, depending on the client's objectives.

3. Use clear, precise, concise, and acceptable language.

Application of law

1. Apply the law correctly to the client's situation.
2. Apply the law comprehensively to the client's situation.
3. Identify any ethical and professional conduct issues and exercise judgement to resolve them honestly and with integrity.

You will not be tested on negotiation in legal research.

What makes good legal research

Good legal research will enable the reader to clearly and easily understand the background to the legal advice being given (the underlying sources of law) and the advice will address the client's issue/s, acknowledging and trying to meet their objectives. Where there are alternative options for action, the advice should be clear on the pros and cons of each and, ideally, recommend which will better fulfil the client's objective/s.

Hints and tips for your legal research assessment

This is not research as you may previously have done it

Given that you are provided with the legal sources you should be considering for the purposes of the assessment, this is not legal research as you may have done it. As advised before, please stick to the way the SRA recommends that meets its marking criteria.

Cover everything that you are asked to do in the instructions

Make sure you cover everything requested in the email from the partner. Whilst the SRA has said there is no specific format for your answer, it is very important that your answer is clearly structured, so it is easy to understand.

You can copy and paste

Remember, you can copy and paste in the Pearson Vue assessment platform – this can be particularly useful for the legal research assessment as you can copy and paste citations from the sources you are using.

Decide how you are going to take notes

Decide how you are going to take notes (see "Try some different forms of note-taking until you find one that works for you," pages 79–80 for some different types of note-taking).

> **TAKE A MOMENT ...**
>
> What are you going to pull out from the documents and how do you plan to record it? For example, client issue/s and objectives, key legal principles etc.

Have confidence in your own judgement

Be decisive in determining what is relevant: at least some of the material sources you receive will not be relevant to the task you have been given. Candidates often struggle with discarding material in an assessment situation. However, you must do this for the legal research assessment and do it quickly. You will get better at this as you practise, and it is important for you to have faith in your own decisions as to what is relevant; do not lose time second-guessing yourself.

Have a strategy for how to treat the different types of research material

For example, there is no requirement to read the research material provided in the order it appears. Some candidates prefer to start with primary sources to get a grip of the underlying law, whereas others prefer to start with secondary sources (especially practitioners' texts) to get the bigger picture.

Legal writing

Before reading this section, please make sure you have read the general SQE2 information at the start of this chapter. This covers SQE2 information that will not be repeated here.

The legal writing assessment

You will have three 30-minute legal writing assessments, one on each day of the written skills examinations. During the legal writing assessment, you will be provided with an email from a partner in your law firm that explains what you are required to do. This instruction email may have electronic attachments. Your task will be to write a letter or email as the solicitor in a matter which clearly and correctly applies the law to the client's concerns. Your writing must be appropriate for the recipient; potential recipients include the client, a third party, the other side in a litigation matter or client transaction, or a partner within your firm. Depending on the fact pattern, your legal writing may be undertaken in the context of a negotiation.

The SRA marking criteria and requirements (these are all taken from the SRA's SQE website)

Assessment objective: You must demonstrate that you are able to produce a letter or an email as the solicitor acting in a matter.

Skills

1. Include the relevant facts.
2. Use a logical structure.

How the communication is structured will depend on what it is trying to achieve, and the audience it is for. Remember you can use headings and bullet points (where appropriate) for clarity and you should be aiming to write in clear, plain English.

3. Provide advice/content which is client and recipient focused.

Keep in mind who the email/letter is for and make sure that you have covered the necessary points in the instruction email.

4. Use clear, precise, concise, and acceptable language which is appropriate to the recipient.

Application of law

1. Apply the law correctly to the client's situation.
2. Apply the law comprehensively to the client's situation.
3. Identify any ethical and professional conduct issues and exercise judgement to resolve them honestly and with integrity.

What makes a good piece of legal writing

Consider this from the point of view of the intended audience. Legal writing should clearly explain what they need to know and if relevant, set out their options or next steps. Everything requested in the instruction email should be covered, including thinking about the bigger picture to provide comprehensive advice or to ensure everything you might require is requested (depending on the intended purpose of the communication). Ideally you should express yourself succinctly, in short, easy to read sentences and with clear conclusions (if required).

The structure should make the writing easy to understand, with appropriate headings and bullet points where necessary (for example, if they would make lists clearer and quicker to read and absorb). However, bullet points and headings must not compromise the detail of your legal explanations – the link between the advice being given and the bullet points or headings must be clear.

Hints and tips for your legal writing

Manage your time

You have a total of 30 minutes in which to read the instruction email, analyse the task, plan your answer, and write it up, adopting a logical structure. You may want to try ten minutes reading and analysing, five minutes planning, with 15 minutes to write up and proofread. You may also want to analyse under particular headings so that you are beginning your write up at the analysis stage (see "Try some different forms of note-taking until you find one that works for you," pages 79–80).

Work through methodically

Once in the assessment, do not be tempted to miss out any of the four stages set out above, as each will build on the previous step. You should also set yourself time markers to ensure you are moving effectively through the four stages. In particular, allow yourself sufficient time to write up your answer, as it is this that will be assessed.

Do not correct small errors at the expense of completing the assessment

You should aim for your writing to be fault-free, but do balance this with the need to submit a complete piece of work in the available timeframe: do not take time to correct non-material errors at the expense of finishing the assessment.

If you can, leave time to check your work

You should aim to allow a small amount of time at the end of the assessment to proofread what you have written.

Prepare a variety of potential structures in advance

You may want to have a variety of potential structures in mind for different communications to enable you to quickly select an appropriate one for your assessment context. For example, writing to a client is likely to follow a different structure from writing to a solicitor representing the other side. However, if you do decide to do this, you need to maintain flexibility and do what is required in the assessment, rather than trying to force one of your pre-prepared formats onto a communication for which it is not a good structure.

The SQE2 oral assessments

We start with some information relevant to all the SQE2 oral assessments, along with general advice and tips to help you tackle them. We then give an overview of each assessment, along with tips for approaching that specific assessment.

How you take them

You will take the SQE2 oral assessments at an assessment centre at the time you have been allocated. You will have two half days of oral assessments, with one interviewing and one advocacy assessment each day, each in a different legal context. Note that you are likely to need to be in the centre for longer than a half day each time as there can be significant waiting time. The advocacy assessments will be in Criminal Law and Practice (Criminal Litigation) and Dispute Resolution contexts, and the interviewing will be in Property Practice (including money laundering) and Wills and Administration of Estates (Wills and Intestacy, Probate Administration and Practice) contexts. You will not know whether you will start with the advocacy assessment or the interview and attendance note/legal analysis assessment until the day of the assessments.

The exam environment for the oral assessments

The exam environment is tightly controlled, you are not allowed to bring anything in unless it is classed as a comfort item, such as a crutch. You can see a list of comfort items on the SRA's SQE website and you should notify the SRA if you require such items as part of the reasonable adjustments procedure. You will be provided with a calculator, a black ballpoint pen, writing paper, and a highlighter in order to undertake the oral assessments. Subject to any agreed reasonable adjustments, you may not use other equipment. The legal analysis/attendance note, which you will write after the client interview part of your oral assessments, will be handwritten. The assessment papers are in hard copy format, and you are permitted to write on them as you see fit. There will be a preparation or base room (where you will prepare for the assessments and write up the attendance note) and separate assessment rooms (where you will undertake the interview and advocacy assessments). You may take any assessment papers provided to you in preparation for the client interview and advocacy assessments into the assessment rooms. There will be clocks in the preparation or base room and in the assessment rooms. Note that watches are not permitted in the assessments.

For what to expect on the SQE2 days, please see "Timelines and what to expect on SQE2 days," pages 122–125 and the SRA's SQE website.

Ways to prepare for the SQE2 oral assessments

Most of the general tips covered for the SQE2 written assessments (see "Ways to prepare for the SQE2 written assessments," pages 79–83) are equally applicable to the SQE2 oral assessments (buddy up and/or form a study group; find a form of note-taking that works for you; timed practice; make sure you plan; speed up your reading; try a timed attempt; ensure your FLK is current; watch for ethical and professional conduct issues, and negotiation; prepare for the logistics; keep calm; and check your work). As you will be handwriting, whilst the advice on not correcting small errors at the expense of completing the assessment is still relevant, the limitations of the online test environment may not be taken into consideration in the same way as for the written assessments.

Practise out loud under timed conditions

Whilst it can feel odd to be rehearsing an interview or advocacy out loud, it is important that you practise the act of speaking the opening and closing (and questioning) elements of the interviewing assessment and your advocacy. It is the only way to test how fast you speak and which words or phrases you find more difficult or might stumble over. You may also find it helpful to record your performance so you can check your body language, presentation and how you come across. Listening back to recordings of your own advocacy submissions or interviews can highlight weaknesses in clarity, pace, or tone. Many candidates use their phones for recording.

Get friends, colleagues, or family to help you

The best practice you can do is as close to the actual assessment conditions as possible. If you can, get someone to play a client or the judge for you. It's helpful if you can get someone who doesn't know anything about the law as your client, as they will ask the sort of realistic questions you might get in the assessment or in practice. Similarly, if you can get someone who knows the law/how judges behave to play the judge, that would be perfect. But any help you can get is better than practising alone!

Practising your handwriting

When was the last time you wrote anything for a sustained period of 25 minutes? Most candidates will need to spend time practising handwriting at speed for 25 minutes at a time. That is the best way to ensure you will be able to make maximum use of the time in the assessments. It is easy to run out of time to complete your attendance note or to finalise your preparation; however, it is easy to time yourself when you practise to try and prevent this.

Interviewing, advising, and attendance notes

Before reading this part, please make sure you have read the general SQE2 information at the start of this chapter and the information relevant to all the SQE2 oral assessments. This covers SQE2 information that will not be repeated here.

The interviewing and advising/attendance note assessment

Unlike the other SQE2 assessments, which are assessed on either an oral performance or a piece of written work, this assessment comprises both:

- interviewing a client; and
- writing an attendance note that contains legal analysis.

You will have two 60-minute assessments, one based on a Property scenario, which you will complete on the first day of your oral skills assessments, and the other set in a Wills/probate/intestacy context, which you will sit on the other oral skills day.

The assessment has three distinct parts, which candidates have reported are held in different rooms at the examination venue:

- Preparation (ten minutes)
- Client interview (25 minutes)
- Attendance note/legal analysis (25 minutes)

The SRA marking criteria and requirements (these are all taken from the SRA's SQE website)

Assessment objective: Demonstrate that you are able to conduct an interview with a client and that you are able to produce an attendance note recording a client interview and initial legal analysis.

Skills

Interview

1. Listen to the client and use questioning effectively to enable the client to tell the solicitor what is important to them.
2. Communicate and explain in a way that is suitable for the client to understand.
3. Conduct themselves in a professional manner and treat the client with courtesy, respect and politeness including respecting diversity where relevant.
4. Demonstrate client-focus in their approach to the client and the issues (i.e. demonstrate an understanding of the problem from the client's point of view and what the client wants to achieve, not just from a legal perspective).
5. Establish and maintain an effective relationship with the client so as to build trust and confidence.

Attendance note

1. Record all relevant information.
2. Identify appropriate next steps.
3. Provide client-focused advice (i.e. advice which demonstrates an understanding of the problem from the client's point of view and what the client wants to achieve, not just from a legal perspective).

Application of law

1. Apply the law correctly to the client's situation.
2. Apply the law comprehensively to the client's situation.
3. Identify any ethical and professional conduct issues and exercise judgement to resolve them honestly and with integrity.

The interview/attendance note assessment may also test your knowledge of negotiation. For example, client-focused advice may include considering negotiation, or setting out potential negotiation outcomes and tactics/strategies.

Preparation (ten minutes)

You will be given a hard copy of your written instructions, typically a one to two-page email from your supervising partner or a secretary. Whilst not guaranteed, it is likely that you will be provided with a small amount of additional paperwork, such as a copy of a short will, Land Registry official copies, an extract from a lease, and/or correspondence relating to the client's matter.

During your preparation, you should:

- familiarise yourself with the facts from the papers;
- identify the relevant law that may apply to the client's situation on the limited facts currently known to you; and
- identify some of the missing facts you may need to ascertain and the questions you may need to ask the client.

TAKE A MOMENT …

It is important to keep an open mind during your preparation: whilst the papers will, to a certain extent, steer you on the subject matter and the legal issues that the client wishes to discuss, it is important not to prejudge any of the missing facts or the client's instructions that will become clearer during the interview. If you ask the right questions, new information could be introduced in the interview that might require you to change your focus, so be prepared for it!

Hints and tips for your preparation

How you prepare, and the type of notes you should make during your preparation, are quite personal and, to some extent, will depend on the information you are given. However, as you are reading your instructions, you may find doing all or some of the following useful on separate pieces of paper:

1. In a probate scenario, drawing a family tree listing the gifts left in the will (see Figure 3.1, based on a sample question published by the SRA).

A diagram like this summarises the will and much of the fact pattern succinctly, and is something you could add to if further information is revealed in the client interview. Ultimately, referring to this in your attendance note might save you time when writing up the attendance note itself.

2. In a commercial lease scenario, drawing a diagram of "who's who" with an overview of the main term details of the lease (see Figure 3.2, based on another sample question published by the SRA).

Having this easy-to-refer-to summary allows you to introduce what you know to the client about the basic terms of the lease early in the interview, which will give you confidence and help to build a rapport with the client, as you will show you have read the papers! Equally, you might just prefer highlighting the relevant parts of the papers and referring to them in the interview instead, although it might be harder for you to find all the essential parts as they won't necessarily all be in one place.

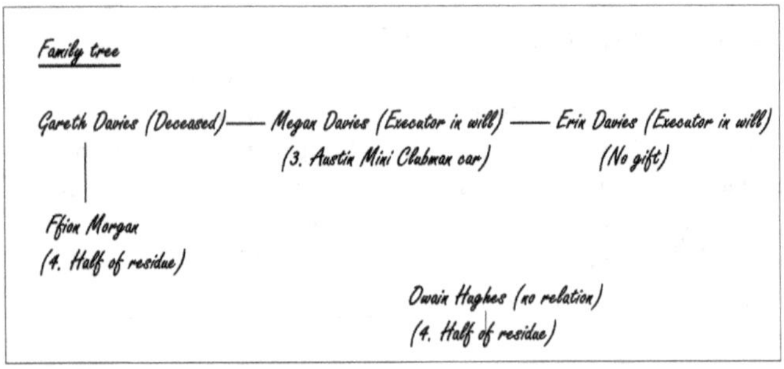

FIGURE 3.1 Handwritten family tree.

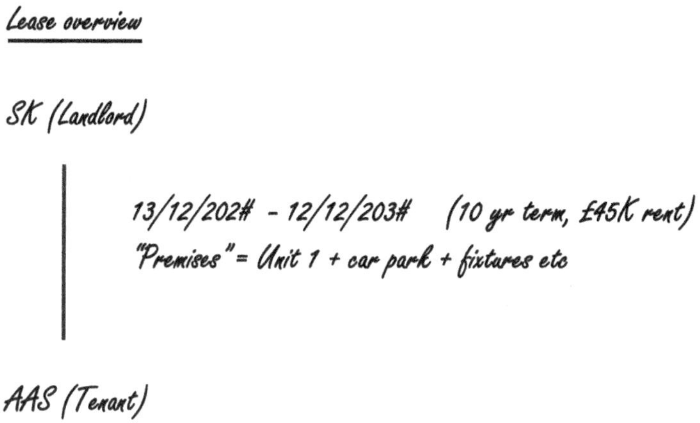

FIGURE 3.2 Handwritten overview of the main lease terms.

3. Writing a timeline of key events (especially if they are not all in one place in the papers).
4. A list of assets and liabilities in a Wills scenario with totals.

> **TAKE A MOMENT ...**
>
> Think strategically about how you use the highlighter you are given in the assessment. Rather than highlighting large chunks of text (which ends up being counterproductive), consider limiting your highlighting to just the key words that you think may be significant, so they are easier to find in the interview and when writing up your attendance note.

Client interview (25 minutes)

This is one of the SQE2 assessments that candidates, even well-prepared ones, fear the most. Why? Because you don't quite know what is going to happen. Other than advocacy, it is the only assessment which requires you to think "on your feet," although you will, of course, be sitting down!

One of the secrets to success in client interviewing is ensuring that you don't just hear what your client has to say (which is purely a passive process), but you listen carefully as well. Listening requires you to be much more active, as it is, ultimately, a cognitive process, requiring you to make sense of what you are hearing in the context of your client's instructions. So, listening in a client interview requires you to be continually asking yourself:

- How does this relate to what my client needs from me?
- What law is engaged?
- Do I need to ask any further questions to fill in the "blanks"?
- What analysis/advice/next steps does this information require me to take?

TAKE A MOMENT ...

It is normal to feel anxious about assessments, especially oral assessments. What techniques will you use to ensure you are calm and able to listen properly to the client?

Hints and tips for your interview

Establish the purpose of the interview

In your preparation for the interview and during the interview itself, make sure you run the interview in a client-focused way and understand whether it is mainly advice your client is seeking, or whether you should be using the meeting mainly to take instructions so you can draft a document at a later date – for example, a will or a lease.

Structure the interview

Structuring your interview in a logical way is key to demonstrating your competence to the person role-playing the client (who will also be your examiner). There are multiple ways to run an effective interview, and to a certain extent, any structure you adopt needs to adapt to the situation. But you might want to base your structure around something like the following.

Introduction/pleasantries

Establish rapport – briefly demonstrate you have read the papers by summarising why you believe the client is here today/some of the key facts. For example:

"I'm so sorry to learn of your brother's death [PAUSE FOR ACKNOWLEDGEMENT/THANKS FROM THE CLIENT]. I note from the papers that you and your sister were appointed in the will as your brother's executors. I believe you would like to know whether you could act as the sole executor and that you would also like some advice in relation to inheritance tax and the distribution of the estate?"

Questions

Start by asking an open question (i.e. one without a "yes" or "no" answer) to establish the full factual background and what your client is seeking. Try not to interrupt them at this stage until they have finished their answer. Then ask open questions to start filling in the gaps (e.g., who else is there in the family – parents, other siblings, other children, grandchildren). End with closed questions to be sure you've understood key parts of the instructions.

Advice

Don't give premature advice until you think you've asked all your questions, although it's always better to ask a relevant question "out of order" than not at all! Then address each of the client's concerns in turn, explaining the legal position in easy-to-understand language – i.e. not like an academic essay. Your advice might need to include the options your client has, in which case, explain them, giving the pros and cons of each, where appropriate.

Next steps/end of interview

During the interview, you should be noting on a separate piece of paper (which you check at this point of the interview) any actions either you or the client need to take after the interview (e.g., your client might have some documents to send you) and the time frames. Usually, it will be appropriate for you to send a letter of advice confirming the advice you have given/the steps you will be taking. Beware! Candidates sometimes forget to list the "next steps" as they are so relieved to have reached the end of the interview! Make sure you clearly denote when the interview has ended, which is a common mistake that similarly exhausted candidates make! For example:

"That completes our interview, unless there is anything further you would like to add?" [PAUSE FOR CLIENT'S LIKELY RESPONSE OF

NO.] "Thank you for coming to see me today. I look forward to speaking to you again soon."

Conduct in the interview room

The assessment starts as soon as you sit down at the desk, so we recommend you start with a simple "good morning/afternoon" after you have arranged your papers as you want them on the desk (no handshake).

In the SRA's sample videos, the candidate says, "I am one of the solicitors at the firm/in the [department name] department." So we recommend you take that approach.

There is no need to take the client's details (name, address, etc.) where the client is an existing client, or where you are told the client is a new client, but all the due diligence has been completed (e.g., money laundering checks).

Keep track of time

You are not permitted to take a phone or watch into the assessment, so as you walk into the room, make a mental note of where the clock is and write down the start time on your rough paper: 25 minutes should be ample. You should expect to spend at the very least 12 to 15 minutes conducting the interview.

You can pause to review your notes

But try not to do so more than a couple of times (maximum) and for no more than a minute at a time, or you may start to lose your rapport with the client. If you do take a pause, which can be helpful to regroup your thoughts, explain to the client what you are doing.

Attendance note/legal analysis (25 minutes)

Once the interview is over, you will write up your attendance note in a different room. It is important to understand that you are aware of the fact that you will handwrite your attendance note, rather than typing it. If you have a medical condition that prevents or inhibits your ability to handwrite for 25 minutes, you should apply for reasonable adjustments in the application you make when you first register for the SQE (see "Requesting reasonable adjustments for SQE assessments" in Part 2, pages 44–45).

> **TAKE A MOMENT ...**
>
> When was the last time you wrote anything for a sustained period of 25 minutes? Like athletes, who need time in the gym flexing their muscles and doing drills to fine-tune their skills, most candidates will need to spend time practising handwriting at speed for 25 minutes at a time. That is the best way to ensure you will be able to make maximum use of the time in the assessment.

Hints and tips for your attendance note

Decide on a format

There is no prescribed format to adopt in your attendance note, but you might find it helpful to work to the following structure:

1. Heading: see Figure 3.3.
2. Brief summary of the client's reason(s) for wanting the meeting.
3. Full factual background: make use of subheadings, where appropriate – for example, when listing the assets and liabilities of an estate.
4. Full details of your client's instructions – for example, if you are asked to draft a document after the meeting, ensure you have details of all the information you need to draft that document.
5. Legal analysis: this should record the definitive legal position of each of the issues raised by the client, using subheadings for each. Although you would not have cited your authorities or used legal

Attendance note of meeting with [name]
Date: [Date of your assessment]
Fee earner: [Your initials]
Client matter name: e.g. Proposed lease of [address] or Estate of {Name]
(Deceased)
Time: [start and end time of the interview)

FIGURE 3.3 Handwritten heading of an attendance note.

jargon in the interview (as your client just wants to know the "answer"), your attendance note needs a more in-depth explanation for any conclusions you reached.

6. Next steps: record what you said (or should have said!) in your interview.

Prioritise correct legal analysis

In legal practice, if you give incorrect or incomplete advice in an interview, to comply with the SRA's Code of Conduct, you would record the advice you gave but then correct anything you need to after the event by email or letter. In the assessment, however, we recommend focusing on getting the legal analysis in your attendance note correct, rather than replicating what you said in the interview, if you believe it was not completely correct. Ultimately, a large part of the attendance note is marked on how well you analyse the legal issues, so there seems little point in spending much (if any) time on what you now consider to be flawed legal analysis.

The SRA does not give definitive advice on whether or not you need to mention that you have changed or added to your advice from the interview. However, in the sample answer to the interviewing and attendance note (probate scenario), the candidate acknowledges misspeaking the "nil rate band" in the interview. This might suggest that you ought to briefly note something along the lines of:

> This analysis expands upon, and in some cases, corrects the original analysis I gave during the meeting, which I would explain in my letter of advice to the client.

This avoids wasting time on incorrect advice, whilst still covering, albeit briefly, the professional conduct issue of clarifying the advice. It is arguable whether you need to state this at all, but it is a suggestion, in the absence of clear guidance from the SRA, particularly if your advice is significantly different.

Use your notes if appropriate

Use your notes from the ten-minute preparation time and the interview if they are helpful.

You can incorporate your notes from your preparation and the interview into the attendance note. You will hand in everything you write, and anything you don't cross out will be marked.

Be careful with bullet points

If you choose to use bullet points or headings, don't compromise on the detail or your explanations, particularly when undertaking your analysis of the legal issues. It is important that the reader can understand the interrelationship between the material in the bullet points, or any headings, and the material they cover.

What makes a good interview and attendance note?

Interview

The SRA has provided two very different types of interviews in the samples it has shared. The Wills example was where the client's main reason for seeing the solicitor was to get some legal advice on a number of issues. In contrast, the primary purpose of the property scenario was for the solicitor to take the client's instructions in relation to drafting a new commercial lease. In the former case, the questions candidates were expected to ask should have been focused on identifying the key facts so they could give the required advice. Whilst the property scenario did require candidates to provide some legal advice, the main focus of the candidate's questions should have been on clarifying the nature of the property and the client's instructions on the key elements of the commercial lease they wished to grant – for example, tenant's repairing covenants, alienation, alterations, rent review (if it had been relevant), and any break clauses.

A good interview recognises the client's objectives early and asks targeted questions aimed at eliciting information to advise on those objectives and/or ensure you have sufficient information to proceed with your instructions (e.g., in drafting a new lease). It also confirms the solicitor's understanding of the client's objectives and includes a comprehensive consideration of the client's issues and options to fulfil their objectives as closely as possible.

Attendance note

A good attendance note needs to accurately capture the client's situation, information, objectives, and concerns. It needs to be clearly written so that relevant information and advice can be found and extracted quickly. It also needs to give your reasoning behind the legal advice being given, so it is easy to see how it relates to the client's objectives and concerns. The merits of any options for the client should be noted, and ideally, a way forward would be recommended with an explanation of why it is preferred in the context of the client's objectives.

Your attendance note should normally end with the suggested next steps, including any client instructions for moving their matter forward.

Check out the SRA's sample questions and answers, which tend to show clearly competent but certainly not perfect candidates. Check out the SRA's performance indicators for more guidance. You can find these on the SRA's SQE website.

Advocacy

Before reading this part, please make sure you have read the general SQE2 information at the start of this chapter and the information relevant to all the SQE2 oral assessments. This covers SQE2 information that will not be repeated here.

The advocacy assessment

Unlike some of the other SQE2 assessments, which are assessed purely on written outputs or client-facing tasks, advocacy is distinctive in that it requires you to demonstrate your ability to think, speak, and respond persuasively in real time. It is one of the few oral skills assessments where you must not only apply the law but also marshal facts, construct arguments, and present them confidently to an examiner role-playing as a judge. For many candidates, this is both exciting and daunting: advocacy is a skill that sits at the very heart of legal practice, yet it is also the assessment where nerves, performance pressure, and a lack of structure can most easily undermine otherwise solid legal knowledge.

The advocacy assessment consists of two 60-minute assessments: one will be in the context of Criminal Practice (Criminal Litigation) (for example, requiring a bail application, a plea in mitigation, or a submission on a point of law).

The other will be in the context of Dispute Resolution, requiring submissions in a civil context (for example, an interim application, case management directions, or an application for summary judgment).

The advocacy assessment has two distinct stages:

- Preparation (45 minutes)
- Oral submissions, during which you may be asked questions by a judge (15 minutes)

The SRA marking criteria and requirements (these are all taken from the SRA's SQE website)

Assessment objective: You must demonstrate that you are able to conduct a piece of advocacy before a judge.

Skills

1. Use appropriate language and behaviour.

This includes: using appropriately formal language, making sure that you use the parties' correct names, correctly address the judge and are clear and confident with your submissions.

2. Adopt a clear and logical structure.

Your submissions should be easy to follow and you should group related submissions on the same point/topic together. Stating the key points you are going to cover at the beginning, then clearly signposting each point and submission can provide a helpful structure. For example; "I'm going to cover three points. My first point, under which I have two submissions is..." If you do decide to use this sort of structure, don't suddenly stop signposting part-way through your advocacy!

3. Present a persuasive argument.

To be persuasive you need to make sensible, clear, legally correct points based on an accurate analysis of the client's situation. Consider which of your arguments are the strongest and should be emphasised and whether there are any weaker arguments on which you want to put less emphasis. Use your presentation skills to persuade – think about your tone, emphasis, and timing. You should speak slowly enough to be clear, but quickly enough to get through your submissions. You only have a short time, so think realistically about how much you can cover.

4. Interact with/engages the court appropriately.

You should be polite and professional, make appropriate eye contact (do not read from a script you've prepared) and be as helpful as possible to the judge. For example, you can check they have received the relevant papers, whether they want a recap of the case facts, and direct them to relevant documents as you mention them or if they ask.

5. Include all key relevant facts.

You need to identify the facts that are relevant from the papers and ensure you can remember or access them during your advocacy. Writing a chronology and/or a list of key facts might be helpful for you.

Application of law

1. Apply the law correctly to the client's situation.
2. Apply the law comprehensively to the client's situation.
3. Identify any ethical and professional conduct issues and exercise judgement to resolve them honestly and with integrity.

Preparation (45 minutes)

You will be given a short bundle of written instructions (such as a memo from a supervising solicitor, notes from a client, or an extract from the White Book or Archbold) and, typically, some key documents (e.g., a bail sheet, a draft order, or evidence).

During preparation, you should:

- Identify the nature of the application or submission required.
- Clarify the client's objective (e.g., securing bail, resisting summary judgment).
- Identify applicable legal principles or procedural rules.
- Extract and organise the relevant facts, noting how you will use them as evidence to support your arguments about the legal principles or procedural rules.
- Draft a short "skeleton structure" for your oral submissions.

Hints and tips for your preparation

Your preparation time is short and precious and you should focus on clear, strong, persuasive arguments rather than trying to cover every single point.

During this time, consider:

Facts: What facts favour your client? What facts might be damaging? How do you anticipate the other side framing them?

Law: Which statutory provisions, rules, or case law apply? While you need not cite authorities in detail, you should know the correct test or principle (e.g., "real prospect of success" for summary judgment; "substantial grounds to believe the defendant would fail to surrender" for bail).

Structure: What is the logical order of your submissions? A numbered or bullet-point outline can help you stay focused under pressure. A common approach is to go through the legal test being applied or the conditions that need to be met before applying them to the facts.

Client goals: What outcome are you seeking and why? How will you persuade the judge that it is fair, proportionate, or procedurally correct? What evidence or law will help you? For example, complying with the overriding objective in the Civil Procedure Rules will be persuasive in a Dispute Resolution context.

TAKE A MOMENT ...

Candidates often make the mistake of over-preparing on legal points whilst neglecting to plan the flow of their submissions. Remember: you will only have 15 minutes to speak. Your examiner is looking for clarity, structure, and persuasiveness, not encyclopaedic coverage.

Oral submissions (15 minutes)

You will make submissions to the examiner, role-playing as a judge, who may ask you questions. This is not a dramatic courtroom performance; the emphasis is on clear, logical, persuasive delivery of your argument.

Hints and tips for your oral submissions

Structure

A clear structure gives your submissions authority. One common framework is:

- Introduction: Who you are, whom you represent, who your opponent is and represents and what application you are making. You may also want to check if the judge has received the relevant papers and whether they want a brief summary of the agreed facts.
- Law: State the applicable test or principle succinctly.

- Facts: Apply the facts to the test, highlighting those favourable to your client.
- Counterarguments: Address and neutralise the likely arguments of the other side.
- Conclusion: State the order you seek and why it is just.

Communication and persuasiveness

Your submissions must be:

- Clear: Avoid jargon, long sentences, or over-complication.
- Concise: Judges want focus, not rambling submissions.
- Persuasive: Emphasise fairness, justice, and proportionality. Judges are often swayed as much by principled reasoning as by technical points.

Professionalism and courtroom etiquette

- Address the judge appropriately (e.g., "Judge" for District Judges; "Your Honour" for Circuit Court Judges; "Sir/Madam" for Magistrates). This is correct at the time of writing, but correct forms of address can change, so please check before your SQE2 sit.
- Speak calmly and with measured confidence.
- Be courteous, even when addressing opposing arguments.

You may be asked to clarify points, respond to challenges, or address the opposing party's likely arguments. This tests your ability to think on your feet and apply your preparation flexibly. The examiner may challenge you with questions or alternative scenarios. This tests whether you can adapt. Active listening and flexible thinking are key – you need to be responsive to what the examiner/judge says to you.

What makes a good advocacy performance

Advocacy in the SQE2 is not about dazzling performance but about demonstrating core professional competence. Examiners want to see that you can:

- Prepare methodically.
- Structure submissions logically.
- Deliver arguments clearly and persuasively.
- Remain professional under pressure.

Like driving a car or conducting a client interview, advocacy is a skill that becomes instinctive with practice. The more you rehearse, the more natural it will feel, until you can focus less on nerves and more on clarity of argument.

Ultimately, strengthening your advocacy skills for the SQE2 is about three things: preparation, practice, and professionalism. Accomplish those, and you will demonstrate exactly what the SRA – and your future clients – need from you: a solicitor who can stand up, speak with clarity, and advocate effectively.

Think of advocacy as balancing on a narrow beam: you must keep your footing by holding onto preparation, clarity, and confidence. Wobbling is inevitable – you may forget a phrase, stumble, or lose your place – but regaining composure and moving forward demonstrates resilience, which is itself a professional skill.

Additional hints and tips for your advocacy assessment

Build a "toolkit" of phrases

Develop a bank of phrases to use naturally, such as:

"Your Honour, I appear on behalf of [client] in this application for bail..."

"The applicable test is whether there are substantial grounds to believe..."

"I respectfully submit that..."

"On the facts of this case, it is clear that..." This avoids hesitation and boosts fluency.

Practise under timed conditions

Like handwriting practice for the attendance note, advocacy requires real-time drills. Practise submissions aloud, ideally in front of someone who can role-play as a judge. Set an alarm so that you know when fifteen minutes have elapsed.

Learn to handle judicial interventions

Practise answering "curveball" questions. Pause, compose yourself, and return to your structure. Avoid panicking or conceding unnecessarily.

Manage nerves

Techniques such as slow breathing, pausing before starting, and keeping a simple written outline can help manage adrenaline. Remember: examiners are not testing theatrical flair but professional competence.

Citing the law

You do not need to memorise case law. You need to know the legal test or principle, but not precise case names or citations. You should only cite statute and the CPR briefly and where relevant (e.g., "under CPR 24.2 the test is whether..."). Do not waste time quoting at length.

Forgetting your argument

If you forget an argument, or otherwise find yourself struggling, move smoothly to your next point. Rambling while trying to remember risks losing credibility.

Using your preparation notes

You may refer to your preparation notes. Avoid reading them verbatim – eye contact and natural delivery matter.

Dealing with judicial challenges

If the judge challenges your submissions strongly, stay calm, acknowledge the point, and respond logically. For example: "Your Honour, while it is correct that my client has previous convictions, I submit that the conditions proposed would adequately address the risk of re-offending."

Use formal courtroom language

Use formal courtroom language, but keep it natural. You are not expected to mimic barristers in the High Court; simply demonstrate professionalism and courtesy.

Before and after the SQE2 assessments

Candidates should complete the pre-booking steps for SQE2 (via the SRA's SQE website) as soon as they receive confirmation that they have passed SQE1. From the day following the release of the SQE1 results, candidates who have submitted a seat reservation form for SQE2 (see below) will be sent requests for payment to confirm their SQE2 place. The candidate must pay within a short time window in order to secure that place.

As for SQE1, candidates who are seeking reasonable adjustments must submit a seat reservation form (whether they intend to sit SQE2 at the next possible sit or later). At the time of writing, payment for places for students with reasonable adjustments is handled outside the main SRA SQE website, and candidates must follow the instructions they have received by email to ensure they pay on time.

As for SQE1, if a candidate did not submit a seat reservation form for a particular SQE2 sit, it is possible that they will be able to book a place at the very end of the booking window if places remain available. However, the uncertainty surrounding this option means it is not the recommended route to take.

The SRA's SQE website is the source of truth for all aspects of the SQE. It is important to regularly check for updates or changes to the SQE regime.

Written assessments

For the SQE2 written assessment days, candidates receive a booking confirmation email in advance that provides the address of the test centre, the time they must report there, the start time of their assessments, and the length of the assessment day.

Accessibility and reasonable adjustments

Students apply for their reasonable adjustments for both SQE1 and SQE2 when they first register for the SQE. Given the different nature of the SQE2 assessments (including the fact that some of the assessments are undertaken in person, face to face), it is important that your application takes account of any adjustments you may need for each part of SQE2 compared with SQE1. The SRA's SQE website provides accessibility information about the venues that are used for the SQE2 oral assessments.

Booking

To a large extent, the booking procedure for SQE2 mirrors that for SQE1 (see "Booking the SQE1 assessments," in Part 2, pages 41–47).

This includes the fact that candidates who need to request reasonable adjustments are outside the standard booking process.

Whilst SQE2 written assessments take place in Pearson Vue test centres in the same way as SQE1, SQE2 oral skills assessments take place in a limited number of venues in England and Wales and must be undertaken in person. This means that many candidates must travel (and potentially find accommodation near the assessment venue) in order to sit SQE2 oral assessments. At the time of writing, SQE2 oral skills assessments were held in Birmingham, Cardiff, London, and Manchester.

One key difference between booking SQE1 and SQE2 is that, whilst you can reschedule your SQE2 written assessments after you have booked (whilst the booking window remains open), rescheduling the SQE2 oral assessments requires you to cancel and rebook the whole of your SQE2 oral assessments via the SRA Candidate Services team. As for SQE1, you cannot make changes to your booking after the relevant assessment booking window has closed.

Fees

The cost of sitting (or resitting) SQE2 assessments has now exceeded £3,000, which you must pay when you book to confirm your place. If, for any reason, you decide to cancel your SQE2 place, you must carefully check the SRA's SQE booking terms and conditions to determine the level of cancellation fee you must pay. The process is largely the same as for SQE1 (see "Mitigating circumstances" Part 2, pages 51–53).

Assessment delivery disruption

In the event of an assessment delivery disruption (or ADD) during an SQE2 assessment, the procedure is very similar to that for SQE1 (see "What if something goes wrong during the assessment?" in Part 2, pages 51–54).

The key difference is that, if you have already attempted part of the SQE2 assessments before an ADD is declared, you must sit the whole of SQE2 again, either at a rescheduled sit shortly after the ADD or in a later sit of SQE2. There is no option to retain credit for only a part of SQE2.

Marking and results

The SQE2 assessments consist of a total of 16 different assessment "stations": 12 of these stations are written assessments and four are oral assessments. For each of the 16 assessments, you will be assessed against the SQE2 assessment specification for the skill in question and against the standard of a just competent day one solicitor.

For each of the 16 assessment stations, you will be awarded marks on a range from A to F:

A = Superior performance: well above the competency requirements of the assessment.

B = Clearly satisfactory: clearly meets the competency requirements of the assessment.

C = Marginal pass: on balance, just meets the competency requirements of the assessment.

D = Marginal fail: on balance, just fails the competency requirements of the assessment.

E = Clearly unsatisfactory: clearly does not meet the competency requirements of the assessment.

F = Poor performance: well below the competency requirements of the assessment.

The marker for each assessment station provides their marks against the assessment criteria for that skill; in each case, some assessment criteria relate to skills and others relate to the relevant law. So, for example, for advocacy, there are skills criteria and law criteria (including ethics and professional conduct). The marker in an advocacy assessment station will, therefore, give the candidate a grade from A to F for each of the assessment criteria. These grades are then converted into numerical marks on the basis that A equates to five marks, B equates to four marks, C equates to three marks, D equates to two marks, E equates to one mark, and F equates to zero. The SRA then calculates the candidates' average mark for each of the skills and the law. So, for advocacy, the skills marks would be averaged together, and the law marks would be averaged together. The final step is that the averages for each of skills and law at a particular station are averaged together to give the overall average mark for that station.

The client interviewing oral assessment works slightly differently from the others. In that assessment, the marker in the interview itself only provides marks against the skills criteria. The attendance note is marked against both skills and law. This means that the whole of the law aspect of the candidate's score is drawn from the attendance note aspect of the assessment. The candidate's skills marks from both the interview and the attendance note are averaged to give the overall skills mark for that station.

Once determined, the scores for all 16 stations are aggregated, divided by 16 (to give an overall average), and then multiplied by 20 (to give an overall percentage). This percentage will appear on your results transcript. As for SQE1, there is no pre-determined pass mark for SQE2. Each candidate receives their result as a scaled score out of 500, with 300 being the pass mark (see "Results and marking" in Part 2, pages 54–57 on how scaled scoring works in practice). This allows the SRA to adjust candidates' marks to take account of differing levels of difficulty between different individual assessments. As for SQE1, candidates are told the quintile into which their mark fell and whether their mark is a PASS or NOT PASS.

Timelines and what to expect on SQE2 days

The SQE2 assessments take place every three months, which provides candidates with more flexibility than for SQE1. SQE2 sits take place in assessment windows that begin at the end of January, April, July, and October in each year, extending into the first two to three weeks of the following month.

The SRA has made it possible for candidates who would like to do this to sit SQE1 and to proceed immediately to sit SQE2 at the next sit. A candidate's ability to do this is, of course, contingent on them having passed SQE1.

The booking form procedure used to book SQE1 assessments is very similar to the procedure used for SQE2 assessments. About four months before the intended SQE2 sit, candidates are sent a seat reservation form that they should complete and return if they plan to sit in the next round of SQE2 assessments. Note that this means that many candidates will submit this seat reservation form for SQE2 before they have even attempted SQE1. Note that there is no cost associated with submitting a seat reservation form and that, if the candidate did not pass SQE1, they simply would not be offered an SQE2 place.

After you have booked your SQE2 written assessment days the SRA will send you an email confirming the address of the assessment centre, the time you must attend (for booking in procedures), assessment start time and the length of the assessment day. If you are late, you cannot enter the assessment so you must ensure you are on time. Make sure you leave enough travelling time for unexpected delays – it is better to be early and have to wait than to be denied entrance and be unable to sit the SQE2.

As for SQE1, candidates will be obliged to register at the test centre and complete ID and security checks before they are able to sit. You must ensure you check your confirmation email for details of any documents you must provide on your assessment days. See the SRA's SQE website for further information on security checks. Note, checks at some centres can include security wanding, so if you are unable to comply with this procedure you will need to apply for reasonable adjustments, explaining why (e.g., medical device that will be affected, or will set off the security wands). If you have to carry a metal or magnetic item for religious purposes, you must contact the Candidate Services Team to inform them. The deadline for submitting all medical or religious declarations is the booking closing date.

On each SQE2 written assessment day, candidates will sit four relatively short written assessments across two sessions. The first session will be one hour and 30 minutes long; there will then be a 15-minute break before a second session, which is one hour and 45 minutes long. Note that, during any breaks, you are not permitted to leave the assessment centre, and you may only access your personal belongings to drink water or take medication. If you will need to take medication you should notify the SRA's SQE Candidate Services Team in advance. No refreshments are provided so you should bring anything you need. The secure space to store your possessions is limited so only bring a small bag. Water is not permitted in the assessment room.

As for SQE1 (and before the start of each individual assessment), you will be obliged to make a fit to sit declaration (see "Are you ready?" Part 2, page 41) and confirm that you accept the confidentiality obligations and assessment regulations for this assessment.

In the same way as for SQE1, you may not take any personal items into the assessments at the Pearson Vue test centres. This includes water, watches, other valuables, notes, and so on. You will be provided with an erasable whiteboard notepad and pen to use during the written assessments.

Once the assessment has started you must remain in your assigned seat until escorted out by a test administrator. In the breaks between assessments, you must leave the assessment room. You will then be required to undertake a further ID check before you re-enter the room. You will be monitored all through the assessments (this can include CCTV).

There is no dress code for the SQE2 written assessments, but it is advisable to wear layers so you can moderate your temperature to be comfortable during the assessments.

As for SQE1, you are not permitted to leave the assessment early. The only reasons you may leave the assessment room during the assessment are to use the bathroom, drink water, eat, or obtain medication. The assessment clock will not be stopped for any unscheduled breaks you take.

On the oral assessment days, the assessments run from 8 am to 8 pm, with individual candidates attending for between 4.5 and 7 hours within that window. When you book, you will receive a confirmation email from the SRA that provides your assessment dates and the exact location of the assessment centre. You will not, however, be told at that stage what time your assessments will take place, so you are advised to assume that you may be required to attend at any time between 8 am and 8 pm on the assessment days. About two weeks before your SQE2 oral assessments, you will be sent joining instructions which give the time at which you must report to your oral assessment centre. As for other SQE assessments, if you do not arrive on time, you will not be permitted to enter the assessments. While the assessments only take approximately two hours a day, you should expect a lot of waiting time.

During waiting time, you will be supervised and light refreshments (hot drinks, water, fruit, biscuits) will be provided, though you can also bring your own cold lunch and refreshments as well (but note that you will not have access to your own belongings once you have put these away in order to start the assessments). While waiting, you can bring and access hard copy materials, but electronic devices (e.g., mobiles, laptops) and bluetooth headphones etc. are not permitted.

On the oral assessment day, you will be required to:

- Leave all of your personal belongings in a secure storage area.
- Register for the assessment day, verify your identity, and undergo security checks (please see pages 47–51, "The practicalities: Before, during, and after the exam" in Part 2 regarding security screening).
- Sign a fit to sit declaration, confirm you understand your confidentiality obligations and that you are bound by the assessment regulations.
- Collect your identification badge, which you must wear at all times when you are at the assessment centre.

Note that once you have undertaken your security checks, you may not leave the assessment centre until you are instructed to do so at the end of the assessment day.

For each oral assessment that you undertake during a particular assessment day, you will have a period of preparation in a preparation room. You will then be escorted to the assessment room by an exam marshal for you to conduct the client interview or oral presentation, as applicable.

After the client interview, a marshal will escort you to a base room to complete the attendance note/legal analysis.

Unlike for all other SQE assessments, water and light refreshments are provided to candidates who are undertaking the SQE2 oral assessments. This is because candidates are not allowed access to their belongings throughout the day.

You may not leave the assessment centre until you are instructed that you may do so. You will not be able to access your personal belongings once you have secured them, water and light refreshments are provided during registration and your scheduled break. Water is available in the preparation and base rooms. If you need more sustenance for medical reasons, you should contact the SRA's SQE Candidate Services Team.

You are expected to wear clothes suitable for a business environment when sitting the SQE2 oral assessments. For example, you may choose to wear a suit or similarly formal clothes, and it is best to avoid casual clothes like jeans and trainers. The SRA advises bringing a warm piece of clothing that is easily removeable (like a scarf) to ensure you are comfortable. You will be expected to stand during the criminal litigation advocacy assessment (subject to any reasonable adjustments).

Mitigating circumstances applications for SQE2

The time limit to apply for mitigating circumstances for the SQE2 assessments is 16:00 UK local time, five working days after your last assessment station. The process to apply for mitigating circumstances is the same as for SQE1 (see "Mitigating circumstances," Part 2, pages 51–53).

The difference with SQE2 is that you will receive the outcome of your mitigating circumstances claim on the same day as you receive your SQE2 results. If your claim for mitigating circumstances for SQE2 is successful, the default position is that the whole attempt will be discounted, and you will be required to resit all 16 assessment stations, the whole of SQE2.

However, in exceptional circumstances, where a claim has been accepted for mitigating circumstances for a single assessment station, and further statistical analysis shows that you could have passed the assessment overall had the event not occurred, the impacted assessment station may be removed and your mark recalculated based on the remaining 15 stations. This could result in you passing SQE2.

As for SQE1, if your claim for mitigating circumstances is successful, you can expect to receive a refund of 75% of the assessment fee you paid for the SQE2 sit. If your claim for mitigating circumstances is unsuccessful, your SQE2 result will stand and will be recorded as one of your attempts on your candidate account.

After the assessment, what happens next?

In view of the complexity of the marking and moderation for SQE2, the results are not published until about four months after the assessments have taken place. For many candidates, this means that they will be in the workplace by the time they receive their SQE2 results.

Tips for getting the best out of your SQE2 experience

Think carefully about where you should book each of the written and oral skills assessments. For the written skills, the factors feeding into this decision will be similar to those you took into account when booking SQE1. For the oral assessments, the range of assessment venues is much smaller, and many candidates must travel to be able to sit. Think well in advance about how you will travel to the venue for your oral assessments and whether, in reality, you will need to find accommodation nearby in order to be able to sit.

Once you have made your bookings for SQE2, you will be able to plan how the assessment period will unfold in your particular case. So, for example, the order in which you will be assessed in the various skills (and which law will be assessed on which days). This will allow you to plan your time immediately around the assessments in terms of refreshing the relevant skill as you approach each assessment.

As for any assessments, try to ensure that you have a good night's sleep before each assessment day and eat and drink healthily. Think about how you might work exercise into your assessment schedule if you find that helpful to allow you to relax and sleep.

Do not be overwhelmed by the number of assessment stations you will encounter during SQE2: each of them is relatively short, and you will be assessed on your average grade over all 16 stations, so you may well be able to pass SQE2 even if you have a poor performance in one or two stations. As much as you can, work on giving your best attempt to each station, then leave it behind so you can concentrate on the next one.

SQE transitional provisions for LPC graduates and SQE2

There are still a number of LPC graduates who have not/will not manage to secure an "old style" LPC training contract. In order to give them the opportunity to qualify, the SRA will, under the SQE's transitional provisions, admit them as solicitors provided they complete two years of QWE and they also pass SQE2 by 31 December 2032. Their route to qualification is illustrated in Figure 3.4.

How have LPC graduates performed in SQE2?

The limited data we have seen from the SRA's SQE2 assessment reports suggest that, generally, LPC graduates perform less well in SQE2 than those who have been through the whole of the SQE regime (i.e. have also sat SQE1).

The challenge LPC graduates face is that, alongside demonstrating competence in the relevant skills, they need to be fully up to speed with both the underlying law subjects and the practice subjects, in which those who have pursued the SQE route will have been recently assessed.

LPC graduates will also need to boost their understanding of some areas of the practice subjects in which they were assessed in less depth on the LPC, such as Wills and the Administration of Estates. If an LPC graduate does not address these challenges, they will find it difficult to pass SQE2, however well they perform the skills.

Even though there is an overlap between the skills assessed on the LPC and the SQE, the SQE assesses them in a very different way. In

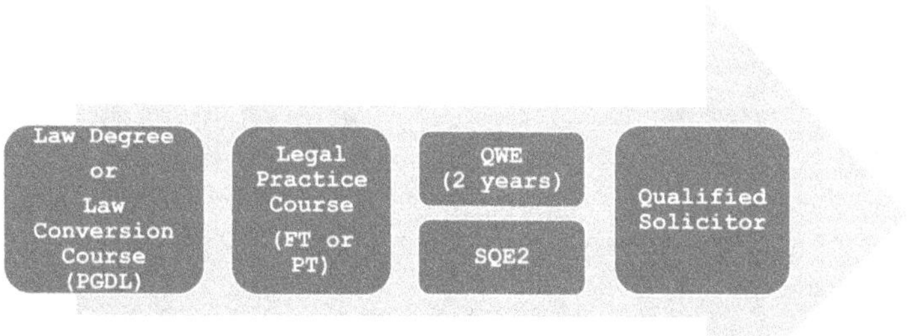

FIGURE 3.4 Transitional LPC pathway to qualification via the SQE.

addition, if you are an LPC graduate already in practice, you cannot assume that the way you are currently performing any SQE2 skill is aligned to passing SQE2.

TAKE A MOMENT ...

If you are an LPC graduate, check the SQE1 and SQE2 specifications in order to undertake a gap analysis to determine which skills and FLK you need to boost in order to maximise your prospects of passing SQE2, first time. You don't want to risk failing and having to pay the hefty SQE2 exam fee for a second or third sit. Only if you are confident in your own ability across all of the written and oral skills should you consider sitting SQE2 without having undertaken an SQE2 preparation course or purchasing SQE2 preparation materials.

4

WHAT'S NEXT?

Starting your career and QWE

Apart from the SQE, what else should you be thinking about to begin a career in legal practice? This section will address recruitment issues, tips, and basic support for professional networking, and offer some suggestions.

QWE

You will recall from Part 1 that, as well as passing the SQE, you need to complete two years of QWE to qualify as a solicitor, which can be accrued:

- in a single, two-year placement with the same employer, like a traditional training contract, or with up to four legal employers;
- before, during, or after your SQE assessments;
- in a single practice area or in a variety of areas; and
- in non-consecutive placements (e.g., you could study for the SQE full-time between QWE roles).

As soon as qualifying as a solicitor becomes a serious aspiration, you should start researching your QWE options. Even if this realisation crystallises in the first year of your law degree or during a non-law degree, it is never too early to start. In fact, we would go as far as to say that for any LLB student, unless you are certain you do not want to become a solicitor, you should be researching the profession and developing a QWE strategy throughout your degree.

So, treat your career as the one module which isn't timetabled, but give it the same time, energy, and focus as any academic module. This means committing three to four hours per week (e.g., an afternoon) researching

DOI: 10.4324/9781003639671-5

the profession and the recruitment process, attending law fairs, webinars, employers' talks, and your university's law society events.

We recommend you start developing your QWE strategy well in advance of sitting the SQE. This will allow you the time you need to give yourself a realistic prospect of securing the right QWE for *you* at the time you want to undertake it. The risk of not planning this is that it will delay the start of your legal career. An associated risk is the temptation to take any QWE you can get rather than planning and securing the QWE that will provide you with the best start to professional life.

Starting your QWE research

Before you begin to research individual legal employers, we recommend that you start by surfing through the many law careers websites that contain extensive resources that support candidates looking for QWE, such as:

- All About Law
- Chambers Student
- LawCareers.Net
- Legal 500
- Legal Cheek
- The Lawyer Portal

On these platforms, you will find resources that will help you narrow the scope of your search – for example, by practice areas, size of law firm/employer, and geographical location. There are profiles of firms and details of the leading experts in particular sectors, all of which will help you to ultimately identify the employers that interest you.

There is also a wealth of information about different sectors within the profession and the practice areas which make up those sectors. For example, you might like the idea of working in corporate law, but only have a limited understanding of what being a corporate lawyer might involve: there are dozens of web pages to guide you on each practice area and subpractice area, with many "day in the life of" blogs by current/recent trainees to add colour to the picture.

Some candidates use a "scattergun" approach: they apply to as many employers as possible in the hope that, eventually, one of those applications might succeed. Our recommendation is to make better use of your time by making fewer, more targeted applications. It is a highly competitive process, so the quality of your application and, critically, the degree to which it is tailored to the firm in question will be essential to your success.

Many successful candidates report that they needed to make numerous applications to secure a role, but each of those applications had to be meticulously researched and targeted to the relevant employer. All law firm graduate recruitment teams have at least one story of applicants sending the same application to different firms with just the name of the firm changed, and sometimes not even that!

TAKE A MOMENT ...

It's the quality of your application that counts, not the quantity of applications you can knock out on a wet Wednesday afternoon. And a quality application relies on a sustained period of thought and research.

Law fairs

Part of your research should include meeting representatives from legal employers at events such as law fairs and employer talks. Most universities host their own dedicated law fairs in October or November each year, and if they don't, they will either pool resources with other local universities and run a joint law fair or promote opportunities in the legal sector at their general careers fairs. *All About Law* and *Legal Cheek* also run large online law fairs, where you also get an opportunity to meet representatives from talent/graduate recruitment teams from law firms, as well as current trainees.

Don't just turn up, eavesdrop on a few conversations, and walk off with bags full of "merch" after a couple of hours. Have a plan!

TAKE A MOMENT ...

Take a strategic approach before attending any law fair. Find out in advance who is exhibiting, research them, and decide what questions you want to ask their representatives. Take a note of everything you hear and who has said it – and not just when *your* questions are being answered. Referencing these conversations could become useful when it comes to creating networking opportunities and for future applications you make.

Getting independent expert advice

As well as doing your research and meeting people who work for legal employers at law fairs, events, webinars, and online workshops, find one or two people you respect with knowledge of the profession you can really trust. This will usually start with the staff at your undergraduate university, although you should be aware that, even if they have practised as solicitors, many law lecturers qualified before the SQE, so their knowledge may be a little out of date. That said, some lecturers in your law school may take special responsibility for employability, in which case you should expect them to be more up to speed. Your best bet, especially if you are studying for a non-law degree, is to start by engaging with your university's careers service. Many universities have law careers specialists who can recommend events and workshops that might suit you and can give you helpful one-on-one advice on the best way to progress to the next stage.

Some of the more well-known SQE providers also provide access to their expert law careers advisers in advance of starting your studies if you accept an offer of a place from their institution on an SQE course.

You may also be able to seek helpful advice on leveraging connections you have made at law fairs (e.g., with current trainees) and with fellow students at your university who may have already secured training contracts.

> **TAKE A MOMENT ...**
>
> Don't be afraid to reach out and ask for help. From anyone. Every successful solicitor had to start somewhere. You will be surprised by how much support is out there. But you do have to be prepared to make the first move and ask for assistance.

One particularly useful source for independent all-round employment advice, coaching, mentoring, and training, particularly for candidates from traditionally under-represented backgrounds in the profession, is Aspiring Solicitors (AS). AS has partnerships with many leading law firms and helps to secure an average of 500 training contracts per year for its members, who engage in a range of programmes and schemes run by expert coaches and advisers, all with one aim in mind: to develop you into the best candidate you can be.

Vacation schemes

For many large City, international, and nationwide firms, as well as some large in-house roles, the recruitment process starts with a vacation scheme (often called a "vac scheme"). You will find these promoted on each firm's website, but you can save a lot of time by checking out the dates of the schemes with most leading employers on the law careers websites mentioned earlier.

Vac schemes typically last one to three weeks at the host employer, who usually runs schemes for around 10–16 candidates several times per year: always over the summer, and often in December and around Easter as well. The schemes do vary between employers, but will often include a combination of most of the following:

- Being seconded to a department each week and being given tasks to undertake to support the lawyers in the team, such as drafting documents and conducting legal and commercial research. Some of this work may be formally assessed.
- Shadowing lawyers at meetings with clients and attending internal meetings.
- Attending presentations by the employer about itself, its practice areas, and clients. Remember, it's not just the vac schemers who want to impress: employers are on a charm offensive to attract the best talent, as the best candidates are likely to receive more than one offer at the end of a vac scheme season!
- Participating in workshops to help develop key skills.
- Preparing presentations with fellow vac schemers before presenting as a team.
- Meeting current trainees: they may present to you and/or you may be paired with one throughout the vac scheme.
- Attending social events and networking opportunities with partners, other lawyers, and important stakeholders working at the employer for you to understand more about the employer's culture and its people.
- It is quite common for candidates to be interviewed at the end of their vac scheme to see how they have reflected on their experience

on the scheme, but of course, in most cases, the employer is going to use any interview to make a judgement on whether they wish to offer you a training contract.

Direct applications

Many law firms and legal employers, especially small to medium-sized ones, have a direct application process instead of, or in some cases, running alongside their vac schemes. Larger employers tend to recruit two years ahead of the start date of your training contract, whereas smaller ones may recruit one year or less ahead of the start of the QWE.

The law careers websites above list the deadlines for direct applications for most medium-sized and large firms. If you aspire to train at one of the smaller firms, it is likely that you will need to go directly to the website of the relevant employer.

Is it best to start your career at a traditional law firm?

Private practice isn't the only career destination for a qualified solicitor. Nor is it your only training option. Training as an *in-house lawyer* (i.e., in the legal department of a large organisation) or in the public sector (e.g., in local or central government or the Crown Prosecution Service) is just one of the alternatives to private practice, which all candidates should be researching and, even better, getting some experience of before settling on their career strategy.

Those working as solicitors outside private practice often report having a higher level of job satisfaction, a better work-life balance, and more robust mental health. Happiness to them would seem like a decent trade-off compared with some of their more melancholic but better-paid peers in private practice.

Whilst these alternative legal careers won't be for everyone, you owe it to yourself to do the research, rather than relying on the recommendation (or otherwise) of someone whose agenda and interests may not be aligned with yours. How do you know you won't like something unless you've *tried* it?

QWE clearing houses

So far, we have focused on QWE at traditional law firms and have mentioned in-house training contracts and roles in the public sector. But, as the SRA anticipated, the introduction of the SQE has led to innovation in the QWE space.

For example, several organisations have emerged, which are, to a greater or lesser extent, part-law firm/part-recruitment agency. Their business models vary: some employ trainees directly and second them to law firms for QWE, whilst others are more like traditional employment agencies. But all have appreciated that legal employers are increasingly looking at more flexible staffing models, with some preferring to recruit part of their junior talent only for short placements as and when there is a business need. So, rather than having to commit to training an individual for a full two years, they may hire a trainee through one of these organisations for six or 12 months at a time – for example, on a specific time-limited project.

The best of these QWE providers make a point of securing good-quality roles for their trainees, so, ultimately, they receive two years of excellent training with up to four employers, which can be hugely beneficial: working in a variety of legal environments can be very instructive as to the type of work and working environment you do and don't like. Also, building strong connections with several employers may be pivotal to securing an NQ role with one of them.

Candidates interested in learning more about these organisations should check out:

- Accutrainee
- Flex Legal
- SQuarE Route

QWE strategy

Having a good academic record, ideally a 2:1 or better, will provide you with a solid foundation for the recruitment process. However, in parallel to working out why you want to be a solicitor and what type of career might suit and interest you, you need to be formulating your QWE strategy.

More particularly, the questions you need to explore are:

- *Do you want to be sponsored by a future employer before starting a two-year QWE training contract with them?*

Sponsors may pay you a maintenance grant during your postgraduate studies, as well as funding your SQE course and exam fees. These employers, who usually start recruiting at least two years ahead of the start date of their training contracts, tend to be the larger City/corporate/commercial/international and national law firms.

Even the least informed SQE candidate will be aware that there is a considerable trade-off which sponsored trainees need to be comfortable with if they accept a training contract at a large firm. On the positive side, the starting salary for trainees at leading law firms (circa £40,000–£65,000 in 2026) and the newly qualified solicitor salary (between £70,000 and £180,000 in 2026) are very attractive. In addition, in most cases, you will have an incredible opportunity to gain experience working in a wide variety of practice areas, often for very prestigious clients. Let's not kid ourselves: at most large firms, there's an expectation that you'll be working into the evenings and some weekends, as and when required. So, you might be earning a tidy sum, but will you get the opportunity to enjoy spending any of it?

More importantly, will you be able to organise your work and personal life so you maintain positive relationships with any life partner, your family, and your friendship groups? Will you still be able to find time to keep fit and pursue your hobbies? Only some trainees at such firms succeed in enjoying a reasonable work/life balance.

- *What do you want to find out about a potential future employer and their QWE/training contract before you make your application?*

There is a wealth of information available on the law careers websites mentioned above, particularly in relation to the 100 largest firms. Regular independent surveys are taken of trainees at these firms, who are asked to rate their training experience in respect of a range of factors, such as:

- *Artificial intelligence and legal technology*: How the firm uses AI and LegalTech and how this affects the day-to-day work of the employer's trainees.
- *Approachability of supervisors*: The experience of trainees will vary from supervisor to supervisor as much as it will between employers. You should be exploring whether your prospective employer has robust, supportive supervision systems in place, as they are essential to optimise your training and development.
- *Client contact*: The amount of client contact will often depend on which department you are working in. As a rule, the larger

the firm and the deal or case, the less direct client contact you are likely to have as a trainee.

- *Corporate social responsibility/pro bono*: Many prospective clients (e.g., on tenders for new work) will require law firms to explain and justify their CSR footprint. In other words, what are they putting back into society/the local community – whether it is pro bono work or dedicated projects to which their lawyers contribute? Good research will reveal the firms that tend to regard CSR as a necessary function of their marketing department, whilst others have more genuine altruistic intentions.
- *Inclusivity*: Employers looking to recruit the best talent are now much more aware than they were ten years ago that being proactively inclusive is essential to attracting both the most diverse and the best pool of applicants.
- *Job satisfaction*: Relatively few of the leading firms featured are ranked highly by their trainees for job satisfaction, compared with mid-size commercial firms, where the feedback from trainees is often more positive.
- *Peer support*: How collaborative is the employer's working environment? Is there a positive approach to "peer to peer" support, or is everyone "too busy"?
- *Quality of work*: Trainees should be given the opportunity to develop the *Solicitor Competencies* during their QWE, and most will aspire to a wide diet of stimulating and challenging work to develop their knowledge and skills. So-called "traditional trainee work" (such as creating bundles of documents for court and indexing of documents), which are more administrative tasks, still must be done, and they will usually fall to the "cheapest" set of hands. So, expect some of this, but in your research, make sure that current trainees aren't complaining about doing too much of these jobs. You are training to become a solicitor, after all.
- *Remuneration package*: The offices of US firms tend to rank the highest for their salaries and remuneration package, but that is reflected in most cases in the hours you are expected to work and the revenue you are expected to generate.
- *Retention prospects*: The likelihood of a trainee being retained as an NQ on qualification. This will vary from intake to intake and will largely depend on the changing needs of the business at any given time. That said, law careers websites do have data tracking back several years, making it relatively straightforward for you to explore the trainee retention record of most medium to large firms in recent years.

- *Secondment opportunities (both international and domestic)*: Opportunities to be seconded for part or all of your QWE/training contract with a client or at an overseas office of the employer.
- *Social life:* It is no great surprise that elite firms don't feature much in a positive way here, but with HR teams having a greater focus on the mental health of their staff, expect to see more non-work initiatives being introduced both inside and outside the workplace to improve wellbeing.
- *Sustainability policy of the employer*: Like inclusivity, a legal employer's sustainability policy is another factor that both clients and future trainees have started to inquire about when making judgements on whether to engage with legal employers.
- *Vacation scheme*: The length and format of these vary widely – see also "Vacation schemes," pages 133–134.
- *Work/life balance*: Not surprisingly, most leading law firms are conspicuous by their absence from the league tables for work-life balance!
- *Working from home policy*: In the post-Covid world, there is a certain expectation amongst a core group of *Gen Z* candidates that they will be able to work from home for several days per week. Legal employers' work from home (WFH) policies vary widely. Many now require an almost permanent physical presence in the office, limiting WFH days to an average of one day per week. The rationale is that you will learn much more by simply being in the office – by watching best practice in action throughout your training. These employers take the view that it is more challenging for their supervisors to give you the same exposure to clients and learning opportunities if one or both of you are not in the office.

Concerns often voiced by Gen Z candidates who want more WFH days are that, since Teams, Zoom, and other similar platforms exist, it really isn't asking much to invite trainees to join online conferences and arrange regular online catch-ups. The problem from the traditional employer's perspective is that their staff need to be more proactive in making online supervision moments happen, which is a challenge in what is already a busy, pressurised working environment. In contrast, with both the trainee and the supervisor in the office for four to five days per week, supervision and opportunities to learn will happen organically, will be easier to arrange, and will therefore take place more frequently.

It's impossible to complete competitive applications for more than a handful of firms in any recruitment cycle, so you need to narrow the field by considering how the firms you are considering perform with respect to, say, six of the above factors that are most important to *you*. Speaking directly to trainees (e.g., at law fairs and via LinkedIn) may help you determine which of the issues are more important to you.

- *If I don't get a training contract at a top firm, will I have "failed"?*

There is a curious bias in some student circles – even "snobbery" – that any self-respecting future solicitor should only want to secure QWE by way of a training contract at a large, prestigious City or international law firm. And should you aspire to anything else, you are somehow "inferior." This is, of course, utter nonsense! But, sadly, a "big job" at a "big firm" is sometimes presented as the only example of what "success" looks like. Our advice to all candidates is to be true to yourself and plan to become the type of lawyer you want to be, rather than the one your peers or perhaps an influential family member might be telling you that you *want* to be. There are many ways of practising law as a solicitor, and you need to find the ones that will work for you and fit in with your life aspirations.

The interest and influence of close family members can be a double-edged sword when it comes to fulfilling your career aspirations. For those fortunate enough to be in such a position, of course, any financial and emotional support is very helpful, but it should never be contingent on the career direction you have to take. We have coached many candidates whose parents wanted a corporate or commercial career for their child, in circumstances where the candidate felt compelled, as a sense of family obligation, to follow that pathway. Those who have the courage to tell their parents that they don't want to work for a City firm are almost all met with the same reply: "We thought that's what you wanted!" And in most cases, after a little introspection, the parents reappraise the goals they have for their child's career and continue to support them in their wish to qualify as a family or human rights lawyer or in another non-corporate/commercial practice area.

> **TAKE A MOMENT ...**
>
> It's your career, no one else's! Even if someone very close to you is helping you financially, make sure that you're following your dream, not theirs. Having a "difficult" conversation now could save you a lot of stress and regret later. And if it means a close family member having to reset the goals they had for you, so be it! You'll be surprised how supportive most of them will be once you explain to them that they may have "misunderstood" your career goals.

Whilst being sponsored will be one of the cheapest routes to qualification, it is not for everybody: practising largely in the corporate/commercial world may be financially alluring, but if deep down you want to be a housing or social welfare lawyer, why start something you don't want to finish? You may get qualified, but then what next? You may find it very challenging to pivot away from the corporate/commercial world, particularly if you have little or no QWE in the practice area you aspire to qualify into.

> **TAKE A MOMENT ...**
>
> Think about your medium- and long-term career goals when formulating your QWE strategy: don't just make decisions based on short-term financial considerations. So, wherever possible, try to start your career with a clear roadmap of where you want to be three to five years post-qualification and how you might get there.

- *Do you have a realistic prospect of securing a vacation scheme and/or employment with a large sponsoring employer?*

Most readers will appreciate that large law firms that sponsor their future talent through the SQE receive bucketloads of applications each year compared with the number of training contracts they are able to offer. For example, the largest intakes at Magic Circle firms are around 100 each year, which are often split between start dates in September and March. There are no accurate records published across the sector, but if some just outside the Magic Circle report having over 2,000 applicants, it is not unrealistic to expect the largest and most prestigious firms to sift through at least 5,000–6,000 applications each year.

> **TAKE A MOMENT ...**
>
> If the chance of being sponsored by one of the largest firms is as little as 2–3%, get advice from expert law careers advisers before you start to seriously commit large amounts of time to applications to such employers. They can advise on your best strategy, the firms to/not to apply for, and how to optimise your applications for vacation schemes and QWE.

If you are advised that the dream is attainable, you will almost certainly need support and guidance with your applications to maximise your prospects of success. Equally, if you are advised that, at least for now, you are very unlikely to secure a sponsored training contract, your limited time and energy are, perhaps, better spent on exploring other pathways and employers in respect of which you can seek further guidance.

- *Do you want your QWE to look like a traditional training contract?* (i.e., typically four six-month *seats* with a single employer, which will give you a wider range of experience in different teams)

Or would you prefer your QWE to focus on just one practice area, so you spend two years training in it and are considerably more experienced in that practice area on qualification than someone who has just done a single six-month seat in such a department? If you choose to narrow your QWE to a single practice area, you need to be 100% sure that this is your "calling," rather than accepting the job because it's the only one currently on the table.

- *When do you want to complete your QWE in relation to your SQE journey?*

The SQE qualification regime is flexible: remember, you can complete part or all of your QWE before, during, or after your SQE studies/assessments. Or combine your QWE with your SQE preparation by studying part-time over a longer period.

Sponsored students are usually instructed by their future employer to study full-time at a specific SQE training provider and complete the SQE before they start their training contract. So, this flexibility is generally only relevant to self-funding candidates. The timing of when you start your SQE preparation will largely be driven by your financial and personal circumstances.

- *Would you prefer to accrue a QWE portfolio with up to four employers over two years so you can get a variety of training experiences at different employers?*

This may be helpful if you're not quite sure where your future legal career may be heading.

Beware the dangers of a QWE portfolio!

Consciously opting for a QWE portfolio strategy can be a wise decision, especially if you are not sure what type of solicitor you want to be and you are recruited by one of the specialist legal recruitment and resourcing firms mentioned previously. However, it is essential to your prospects of securing a good quality *NQ* role that most (if not all) of the placements you complete across your portfolio fit together in a way which "tells" a future employer that you are a serious candidate for the role you are applying for. In other words, in an ideal world, most (if not all) of your training needs to align with their practice areas. If, on the other hand, your QWE is a patchwork of any role you could get, you become a much less compelling candidate, as your QWE placements will lack any logical cohesion or sense of career direction.

The reality is, even if they qualify as solicitors, those who default into a mixed QWE portfolio by taking any QWE they can secure just to qualify seriously risk being told by prospective employers that their QWE isn't "good enough." This may be because the candidate's experience lacks the breadth and depth the employer expects of a "day 1" NQ. Consequently, many NQs like this will find it incredibly challenging to progress into quality NQ roles and risk languishing in a succession of further paralegal roles. Or, worse still, some will end up leaving the profession altogether.

Sadly, even if they pass the SQE, many of these candidates will come to regret not having taken a more strategic career plan earlier in their qualification journey. Why? Because a pass in the SQE doesn't guarantee you anything! So, deferring your QWE strategy until after you pass the SQE is not recommended!

But it doesn't mean you can only start the SQE once you have secured your QWE. Not at all! Good law schools that deliver SQE programmes will have great connections with the profession and well-resourced law careers teams, who can enhance your prospects of securing good-quality QWE/training contract roles. So, make sure you have a plan, that you understand the risks, and appreciate that deferring the career plan isn't a plan at all!

TAKE A MOMENT ...

Don't be that SQE candidate who naively thinks that it's OK to put off planning your training and *newly qualified* strategy until a later date. Start thinking about it now if you haven't already! Have a coherent plan that maximises your prospects not just of qualifying but also of securing a good-quality newly qualified role.

QWE FAQs

1. *What counts as QWE?*

Real life (not simulated) work which substantially includes the provision of legal services in which you have had the ability to develop at least two of the SRA's solicitor competencies.

We recommend you keep a contemporaneous record of the work you do by completing the SRA's training template (which you can download from the SRA's website), as it will make your QWE easier to review for the person signing it off, as well as for the SRA.

It isn't the label of the job that counts; it is the work you do. So, paralegals, legal clerks, and legal secretaries may be undertaking QWE when providing legal services where they have the opportunity to develop at least two of the SRA's solicitor competencies. These include:

- *Ethics, professionalism, and judgement* – for example, applying understanding, critical thinking, and analysis to solving problems, such as "assessing information to identify key risks."
- *Technical legal practice* – for example, "drafting documents which are legally effective and accurately reflect the client's instructions, including being able to draft documents from scratch as well as from a legal precedent."
- *Working with other people* – for example, establishing and maintaining effective professional relations with clients, such as "identifying possible courses of action and their consequences and assisting clients in reaching a decision."
- *Managing yourself and your own work* – for example, keeping, using, and maintaining accurate, complete records such as "complying with confidentiality, security, data protection, and file retention and destruction requirements."

2. *Can work undertaken outside England and Wales count as QWE?*

In theory, yes, which partly explains why certain qualified lawyers in overseas jurisdictions are exempt from QWE. For overseas QWE to "count," as with all QWE, it must be signed off by an English and Welsh qualified solicitor (or the legal employer's Compliance Officer for Legal Practice (COLP) if the firm is regulated by the SRA). However, sometimes getting the international QWE signed off locally can be impossible.

Fortunately, there are now some independent English and Welsh qualified solicitors whose businesses charge fees for signing off external QWE where candidates can provide sufficient evidence of the work they have undertaken and have received corroboration of the same from the lawyers who supervised the candidate. Their fees vary widely, and perhaps the SRA does not keep as close an eye on these firms as some of us would wish. We would recommend engaging only with organisations that can demonstrate a long list of strong testimonials from clients who have had their QWE approved by the SRA.

3. *Can QWE be signed off retrospectively?*

Yes, and there is no time limit for how long ago the work was undertaken. However, from a practical perspective, the older the QWE is, the more challenging it may be for the candidate to provide sufficient evidence of what they have undertaken and get it signed off.

4. *Can firms refuse to sign off QWE?*

Some firms were initially reluctant to sign off on paralegals' QWE because they took the view that it diluted the currency of their much sought-after training contracts. However, this is now less of a problem because any employer or COLP who refuses to sign off QWE in circumstances where it meets the SRA's QWE criteria may be subject to disciplinary action. However, the SRA has stated that it will not compel a firm to sign off on a person's QWE or mediate in the event of a dispute.

5. *What is the process for QWE being signed off and approved by the SRA?*

It must be signed off by the legal employer's COLP or a solicitor qualified in England and Wales, who will usually be employed by the legal employer (or a partner). They need to review your work, get feedback from any other supervisors, and confirm:

- the length of the QWE (this may be less than two years if you have accrued the QWE with more than one employer);
- that the work you have undertaken has given you the opportunity to develop some of the solicitor competencies; and
- there are no issues concerning your character and suitability to become a solicitor, but that does not extend to deciding whether you are competent to practise, as that has already been assessed by your passing the SQE assessments.

Once your QWE is signed off, you can register your QWE and apply to be admitted as a solicitor via your mySQE account.

Applying to be admitted as a solicitor

Once you have passed the SQE and had your QWE signed off, in most cases, your admission as a solicitor should be a formality. After checking your SQE and QWE record and/or any exemptions you might have claimed, the SRA undertakes checks as to whether you are a "fit and proper person" to practise, such as checking whether you have a criminal record and whether your character or suitability could otherwise be called into question by any other past conduct or behaviour.

Past indiscretions that may put your qualification at risk are not limited to criminal behaviour, but the SRA will consider each case on its own facts. In particular, academic misconduct (e.g., cheating in exams) may put your qualification in jeopardy. Examples of other past non-criminal conduct which could also be a problem include:

- Violent, aggressive, dishonest, or discriminatory behaviour;
- Insolvency – for example, your personal bankruptcy, entering into a voluntary arrangement with your creditors, or similar insolvency issues relating to any company you have controlled;
- Other financial problems – for example, if your home has been repossessed by a lender;
- Adverse findings (e.g., being disciplined) by a regulator; and
- Disqualification as a director or charity trustee.

The SRA's character and suitability test is governed by the Assessment of Character and Suitability Rules and the SRA Authorisation of Individuals Regulations. If you are concerned that the SRA may take a negative view of something in your past and refuse your application to be admitted to the roll of solicitors, it is best to be open about this with the SRA before you commit to the time and expense of an SQE journey.

Rule 5.2 of the SRA Authorisation of Individuals Regulations gives concerned candidates the ability to apply to the SRA for a provisional assessment of their character and suitability. However, any such assessment will only be indicative and will not be binding on the SRA as and when such candidates apply to be admitted. But at least such candidates can secure a realistic steer as to the SRA's position before embarking on the SQE.

Reflection and professional practice skills

Being a lawyer is surprisingly little about the law itself. To be successful, you need numerous other skills, from diligence and attention to detail to emotional intelligence, commercial understanding, and enthusiasm – not to mention tact and delicacy when delivering advice clients don't want to hear! To develop these non-legal attributes, you need to be a reflective practitioner – you need to think about how you practise your profession. You'll need to identify what works in certain situations, what doesn't, and what you need to do to improve your practice.

Why soft skills aren't soft: The need for professional skills, attitudes, and behaviours

Law firms list the key skills and attributes they expect their employees to have, and the Law Society has a whole set of online learning modules dedicated to non-legal skills and attributes. O Shaped (a group set up to promote the non-legal attributes needed by solicitors and endorsed by numerous legal professional education providers and law firms of all shapes and sizes) lists 12 different attributes/skills under the three headings of building relationships, creating value, and adaptability, as well as endorsing the "O" attributes of open, ownership, optimism, opportunity, and original. (www.oshaped.com).

Given the acknowledged importance of these skills and attributes, labelling them as "soft" seems outdated; it's better to think of them as "essential." They are what enable you to progress your career, work with colleagues, and attract and keep clients. They are how you add value to your firm, whether it is through bringing in work, spotting efficiencies in processes and procedures to make everyone's lives easier, or managing and training the next generation of law firm leaders.

So how do you develop these essential skills and behaviours?

The importance of reflection and some examples of reflection frameworks

This is where reflection and being a reflective practitioner become important. Reflection is the process where you think analytically about your practice and yourself and gain insight into what you are currently doing, what works, what doesn't, and therefore, what you might want to do differently. It's a continual process, as you work at constantly improving what you do and how you do it, and add to or change your skills, behaviours, and attitudes. You should also ask yourself whether your attitudes are helpful and whether the work you are trying to do suits your desired lifestyle and supports your values.

There has been a lot of work done that shows if you have to act in ways that do not reflect your personality or do work that doesn't align with your lifestyle or values, it is likely to cause you significant stress and, as a result, unlikely to be sustainable. Reflection can help you to identify how you can thrive within your role, as well as how you can be better at it.

Different people have different preferred methods of reflection – some people like to reflect in a free-form way, without specific questions to answer, and some prefer a more structured approach. If you are just starting out with reflection, using a structured process can be beneficial, and even if you have your own process, you may want to experiment with different methods to see what works best for you. There are lots of different reflection frameworks. We've outlined three popular ones you might want to try below. Remember, reflection only works if you are honest about what happened and your thoughts and feelings about it. While this can sometimes be difficult, you will get the best results if you are honest and if you try to take a more objective approach – for example, don't just think about things you didn't do well or areas to improve. Think about areas where you are performing well as well.

Driscoll's reflective learning cycle (2007)

Perhaps the simplest reflective framework (Figure 4.1), the stages are outlined below.

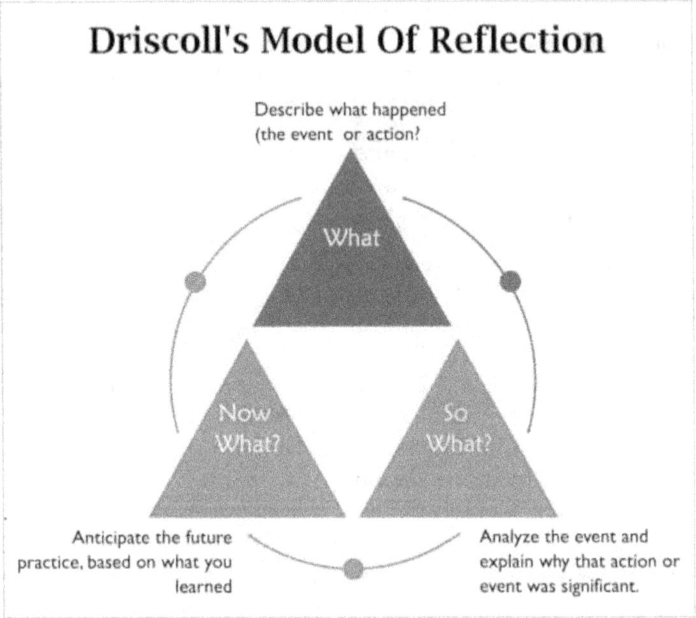

FIGURE 4.1 Driscoll's reflective cycle.

Credit: Shutterstock.

1. What? What happened – describe the occurrence or experience, for example, "I got a low mark in my formative assessment."
2. So what? I am unhappy with the mark and want to do better in the summative assessment.
3. Now what? I need to understand why I got the low mark and make a plan to do better in the summative assessment. What was the feedback and what sources of help do I have? What practical steps do I need to take?

Kolb's experiential learning cycle (1984)

Kolb put forward the theory that the best way to learn is by experience, and his cycle is built on the foundation of "an experience." It has four stages, as you can see in Figure 4.2.

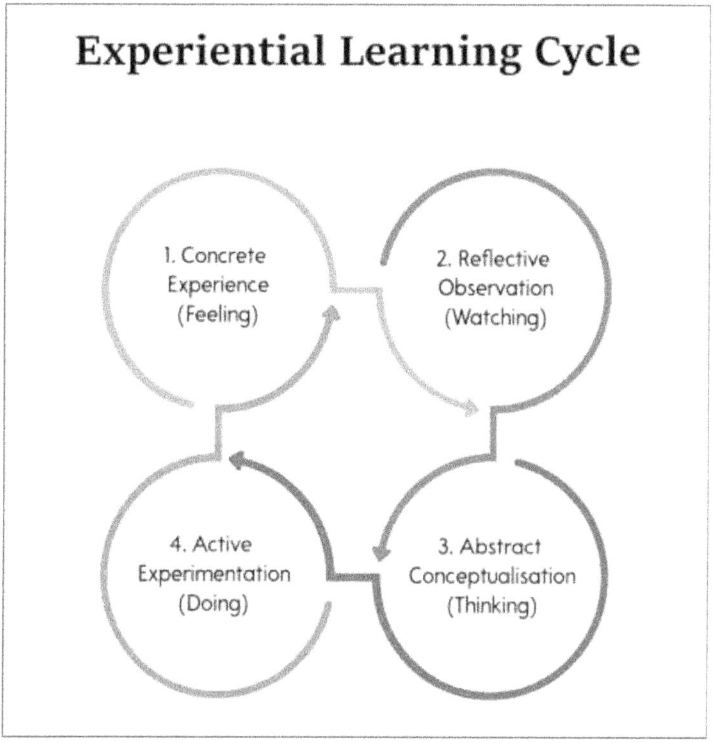

FIGURE 4.2 Kolb's experiential learning cycle.

Credit: Shutterstock.

1. Concrete experience – an actual experience, situation, or series of events. What happened? Who was involved? What was the outcome?
2. Reflection – thinking about what happened and why and how it happened.
3. Learning from the experience – how has this experience affected you and others? What was the event's impact? How might you want to change your skills, actions, and behaviours to improve the event or similar events you may be involved with in future?
4. Action – you can then try any actions you've decided on (we recommend no more than three changes, and you may only want to

make one at a time to check its impact) and run through the cycle again. You can keep repeating the cycle until you are satisfied with what happens during the experience.

Gibbs' reflective cycle (1988)

Gibbs' reflective cycle is a more involved process with six stages. It explicitly takes into account your feelings and encourages a more objective analysis (Figure 4.3). Each stage has some helpful questions to help you reflect.

1. *Description of the experience*

    - What happened?
    - Where did it happen?
    - When did it happen?
    - Who was there?
    - What did they do?
    - What did you do?

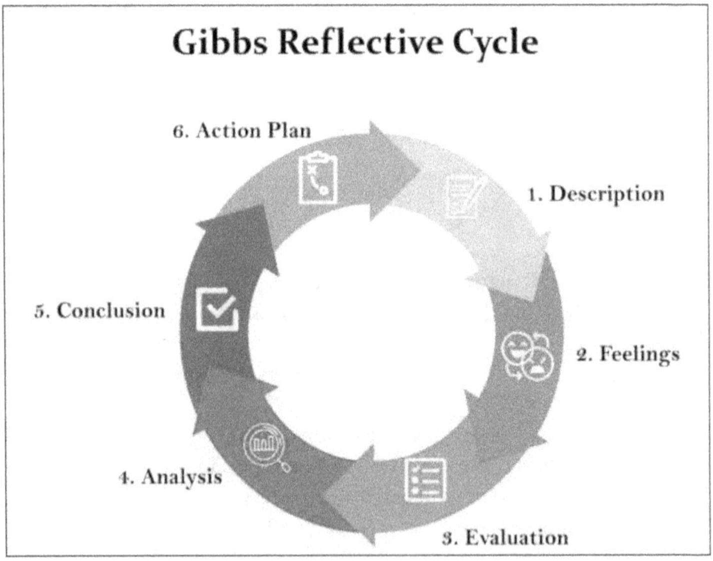

FIGURE 4.3 Gibbs reflective cycle.

Credit: Shutterstock.

- What was the outcome?
- What did you want to happen?

2. *Your feelings and thoughts about the experience*

- What were you feeling during the experience?
- What were you feeling before and after?
- What do you think other people were feeling?
- What do you think they feel about the experience now?
- What were you thinking during the experience?
- What do you think about it now?

3. *Your evaluation of the experience*

- What was good and bad about it?
- What went well?
- What didn't go well?
- What did you and other people contribute to the experience (positively or negatively)?

4. *Your analysis of the situation*

- Why did things go well?
- Why didn't it go well?
- What sense can you make of the situation?
- What knowledge – your own or others (e.g., feedback) – can help you understand the situation?

5. *Conclusions*

- What did I learn from this experience?
- How could this have been a better experience for everyone involved?
- What behaviours, skills, and attitudes do you need to develop to handle a similar experience better?
- What else could you have done?

6. *Your action plan*

- What would you do differently if you had to go through the experience again?

- How will you develop the required behaviours, skills, and attitudes you need?
- How will you make sure that you act differently next time?

> **TAKE A MOMENT ...**
>
> Do you already have a way of reflecting that works for you? How often do you reflect? If not, is it something you think you can incorporate into your life?

Process of continual enhancement

Ideally, reflection is something you would do regularly to continually enhance whatever it is you are reflecting on. For example, you may want to improve your professional email skills because you don't have much experience with using email professionally. Each work email you write and receive is then potentially something to reflect on to analyse whether it works well or not, and therefore what you may want to change about your own professional email writing.

You may have heard of the Japanese word "Kaizen," which is the philosophy and practice of continuous improvement by making small, incremental changes over time. Originally used in Japanese industries, it has been used by the British Olympic Cycling team to great effect ("marginal gains") and is something you might like to try to improve your own skills, attitudes, and behaviours, in conjunction with adopting reflective practice.

By making small, sustainable changes, you avoid the risk of attempting to make significant changes, which either may not yield the result you want or are unsustainable. Having said this, if you are in a situation where you feel a large change is the best way to support your goals, then, as long as it is realistic, it may be a sensible option.

Skills gap analysis

As you progress in your studies, career, and life, you are going to need different skills to tackle different responsibilities. For example, if you end up managing a team, you are going to need to know how to manage people, something that may not have been relevant for you before.

One of the most powerful things you can do to ensure you succeed in whatever you are trying to achieve is to reflect on the skills you currently have and think about what additional skills you need to improve or develop to meet your goals. This is known as "skills gap analysis." You may have heard of it in the context of organisations as well, where a business works out what sort of skills its employees need to support its strategy. This is the same process, just on an organisational rather than an individual level.

A skills gap analysis requires a slightly different type of reflection. Rather than building on an experience you have had, you need to think about the skills, attitudes, and behaviours you need for your goal and then reflect on whether you currently have them, and at the right level for what you want to achieve. If you do not, you need to reflect on how you intend to develop them and over what timescale. Again, being honest with yourself will significantly help this process. Please also see "sources of support."

Sources of support

While reflection can be a completely personal process, it can also help to discuss your reflections with people whose judgement you trust and whom you feel know you well. They can often offer helpful new perspectives or help you be more objective about what you do well (as we tend to dwell on the things we think we need to improve).

You may also have more formal evaluations, like work appraisals or feedback on your studies. It's important to approach any feedback with an open mind and to evaluate whether you think it is useful. If so, then you can use it to help shape your action plan going forward. If you feel it is not accurate or useful, you can always ask the feedback giver for more details to help you make use of their feedback. However, do consider whether to ask and how you are going to ask carefully – for example, a very busy lawyer is likely to give you a better response if you find a time when they are less busy or offer to wait until they can make time for you.

When you have identified skills, attitudes, and behaviours you want to develop and/or change, then you will need to identify how to go about this. There are many free online resources available; for example, a lot of the Law Society's learning for junior lawyers and your place of study or employer may have some specific training or options you can use, such as LinkedIn Learning.

Lifelong learning

Lastly, we wanted to mention lifelong learning. One of the most fantastic things about a legal career is that there is always something new to learn. Throughout your career and hopefully your life, you will be able to take up the opportunities to keep learning and increasing your skills, as well as building new ones. There are so many different roles and paths a legal career can encompass, and it is important that you find what you are interested in and what is right for you, so that you will have the interest and enthusiasm to continue to learn throughout your career.

Career development after the SQE

Passing the SQE is not just about exams – it's about stepping into your future as a solicitor. Preparing for and succeeding in the SQE can feel all-consuming, but it's equally important to lift your head up and think about where you want to go next. Career development is not something to "put off until later." It's an ongoing process that will help you make the most of your qualification and give direction to your efforts.

Why you need to manage your career

Your career won't manage itself – and neither will anyone else. In the legal profession, being proactive about your direction is essential. Managing your career means understanding where you are, identifying where you want to go, and taking deliberate steps to get there. Whether your goal is to work in private practice, the public sector, or academia, developing self-awareness and a clear sense of purpose helps you to make informed decisions. Remember: opportunities rarely arrive fully formed – they are built over time through choices, relationships, and reflection. The legal profession is competitive and constantly changing. Simply qualifying is no guarantee of progression or job satisfaction. By taking charge of your career development, you:

- Build clarity about what roles and practice areas interest you.
- Position yourself strongly for opportunities by aligning your skills and experiences.
- Avoid drifting into areas of law or working environments that don't suit you.
- Create resilience against inevitable setbacks – because you'll have a plan and perspective.

Short-, medium-, and long-term planning

Career planning works best when broken down into time horizons:

- Short-term (next 12 months): Focus on securing Qualifying Work Experience, identifying skills gaps, and gaining exposure in practice areas that interest you. Set realistic and measurable goals, for example, "Draft five attendance notes under supervision by the end of my seat."
- Medium-term (1–3 years): Build specialist knowledge, develop professional networks, and refine your practice area preferences. Broaden your experience and professional network. Seek opportunities such as paralegal roles, pro bono work, or early stage training contracts. Start identifying specialisms or areas of law that genuinely interest you. This might involve applying for NQ roles or moving between practice areas until you find the right fit.
- Long-term (3+ years): Consider where you want to be – partner track, in-house counsel, legal aid, niche specialism, or perhaps an alternative legal career. Long-term planning is flexible, but having a vision gives meaning to your day-to-day work.

Review your plan regularly and adjust your path as your circumstances and ambitions change.

Job hunting

The SQE opens doors, but finding the right role requires strategy. Job hunting can feel daunting, but preparation makes a huge difference. Tailor your CV and cover letter to each role and highlight both technical and transferable skills. Use every opportunity – LinkedIn, alumni networks, local law societies – to connect with others. Informational interviews can provide insight into a firm or area of law, even if no role is currently advertised. Remember: applying for jobs is a skill in itself – practice improves performance. Think about the following:

- Tailoring your applications: Highlight SQE-specific skills, such as client interviewing, legal writing, and advocacy.
- Showcasing QWE: Employers want to see evidence of competence, not just theory. Record your experiences carefully and align them with the SRA's competencies.

- Using multiple routes: Traditional law firms, in-house legal teams, government bodies, and alternative business structures are all options. Don't limit yourself unnecessarily.
- Resilience: Rejections are part of the process. Treat each as feedback, not failure.

Communities of practice and support

You are not on this journey alone. Law is a collaborative profession built on networks of learning and practice. Engage with communities of practice – groups of people who share your professional interests or specialism. These might include:

- Law Society divisions and regional law societies.
- Specialist networks (e.g., Women in Law, Society of Asian Lawyers, LGBTQ+ legal networks).
- LinkedIn groups or online forums for SQE candidates and junior lawyers.
- Pro bono networks and legal clinics, where you can gain experience and contribute.

Being part of a community creates opportunities to learn from others' experiences, share your own challenges, and even find job openings through informal channels.

Linking back to skills gap analysis

Earlier in your SQE preparation, you may have carried out a skills gap analysis – identifying where you were strong and where you needed development. Revisit this exercise after the exam. Your skills gap analysis is a vital tool for career development. Identify where you currently are versus where you want to be, and use this insight to set priorities. If your analysis shows a gap in negotiation or client communication, seek roles, shadowing opportunities, or short courses that build those skills. Revisiting your gap analysis helps ensure your professional development remains purposeful and aligned with your goals. Your legal knowledge will now be sharper, but what about practical skills?

For instance:

- Do you need more experience in drafting commercial documents?
- Are you confident with client communication under pressure?
- Could your advocacy be improved through a local mooting society?

Use your career development plan to target these gaps. Employers value self-awareness and evidence that you're actively working to improve.

Sources of support

Support can be *formal* or *informal*:

- Formal mentors: Found through structured schemes at firms, universities, dedicated support organisations such as Aspiring Solicitors or professional bodies.
- Informal mentors: Colleagues, supervisors, or even peers who are a few years ahead in their journey.
- Supervisors: During QWE, supervisors play a crucial role in shaping your skills – don't be afraid to seek feedback regularly.

Remember, mentors don't need to have all the answers. Sometimes their role is simply to ask the right questions and help you reflect.

Do not be afraid to ask

Law can feel intimidating, and many candidates hesitate to ask for clarification or guidance. But asking questions is a strength, not a weakness. It demonstrates curiosity, commitment, and a desire to learn. Employers would much rather you ask early than struggle silently or make avoidable mistakes.

Adapt as necessary

Your career will rarely follow a straight line. Opportunities arise unexpectedly, and sometimes your interests will shift. Be prepared to adapt your plan as circumstances change. For example, you may discover a passion for in-house work during a secondment, or decide you want a better work-life balance in a smaller firm. Flexibility is key.

Avoid burnout: A call back to resilience

Make resilience a habit. Ambition is important, but so is sustainability. The pressure to achieve can sometimes lead to burnout, especially during demanding periods such as SQE preparation or early practice. Building resilience means pacing yourself, setting boundaries, and maintaining balance. Reflect regularly on what energises you and what drains you, and make space for rest, exercise, and personal interests. A long, successful career depends on wellbeing as much as performance.

- Set boundaries around working hours where possible.
- Keep up hobbies and relationships outside law.
- Acknowledge progress.
- Be happy with excellence, not just perfection.

Remember: you've already demonstrated resilience by completing the SQE. Carry that same mindset into your career.

Top three tips for career management

1. *Remember, people talk – build your reputation through integrity.* How you treat colleagues and clients will shape how others see you far more than grades or job titles.
2. *Avoid all-or-nothing thinking.* Careers are not linear or perfect. Every experience – successful or not – teaches you something valuable.
3. *Know what's in it for you.* Each opportunity should offer one (or more) of the following:

- Learning: Does it stretch or develop your skills?
- Money: Does it meet your financial needs?
- Networks: Will it connect you with people who share your interests or can open new doors?
- Experience: Will it strengthen your CV or help you test a new area?
- Stepping stone: Can it lead to a future role you want?
- Helping colleagues: Does it contribute to a supportive professional community?
- Job satisfaction: Will it bring you purpose and enjoyment?

A successful career is rarely a straight line – it's a journey of learning, connection, and growth. Manage it actively, ask for help when needed, and celebrate each step along the way.

Takeaway – career development is not an afterthought once you pass the SQE – it's the natural continuation of your journey. Manage your career deliberately, connect with supportive communities, adapt as you go, and protect your wellbeing along the way.

Top three tips for career management – remember, people talk, nothing is perfect; try and avoid all-or-nothing thinking; and what is in it for you – learning, money, networks, experience, stepping stone, helping colleagues, and job satisfaction.

REFERENCES

Driscoll, J. (2007) *Practising clinical supervision: A reflective approach for healthcare professionals*. 2nd edn. Edinburgh: Bailliere Tindall Elsevier.

Gibbs, G. (1988) *Learning by doing: A guide to teaching and learning methods*. Oxford: Further Education Unit, Oxford Brookes University.

Kolb, D.A. (1984) *Experiential learning: Experience as the source of learning and development*. Englewood Cliffs, NJ: Prentice Hall.

INDEX

For Product Safety Concerns and Information please contact our EU
representative GPSR@taylorandfrancis.com
Taylor & Francis Verlag GmbH, Kaufingerstraße 24, 80331 München, Germany

www.ingramcontent.com/pod-product-compliance
Lightning Source LLC
LaVergne TN
LVHW052157220926
848675LV00027B/296

* 9 7 8 1 0 4 1 0 7 2 6 8 3 *